HOLOCAUST AGENDAS, CONSPIRACIES AND INDUSTRIES?

HOLOCAUST AGENDAS, CONSPIRACIES AND INDUSTRIES?

Issues and Debates in Holocaust Memorialization

JUDITH E. BERMAN
University of Western Australia

Foreword by
WILLIAM D. RUBINSTEIN
University of Wales, Aberystwyth

VALLENTINE MITCHELL
LONDON • PORTLAND, OR

First published in 2006 in Great Britain by
VALLENTINE MITCHELL
Suite 314, Premier House, 112–114 Station Road,
Edgware, Middlesex HA8 7BJ

and in the United States of America by
VALLENTINE MITCHELL
c/o ISBS, 920 NE 58th Avenue, Suite 300
Portland, OR 97213-3786

Website: http://www.vm.books.com

British Library Cataloguing in Publication Data
Berman, Judith E.
  Holocaust agendas, conspiracies and industries? : issues
  and debates in Holocaust memorialization
  1. Holocaust, Jewish (1939–1945) – Anniversaries, etc. –
  Cross-cultural studies 2. Holocaust, Jewish (1939–1945) –
  Historiography – Cross-cultural studies
  I. Title
  940.5'3186

ISBN 0-85303-711-6 (cloth)
ISBN 0-85303-712-4 (paper)

Library of Congress Cataloging-in-Publication Data
A catalog record has been applied for

Typeset by FiSH Books, Enfield, Middx
Printed in Great Britain by MPG Books Ltd, Bodmin, Cornwall

Contents

Abbreviations

AJH	*Australian Jewish Herald*
AJN	*Australian Jewish News*
AJN (Melb.)	*Australian Jewish News* (Melbourne edition)
AJN (Syd.)	*Australian Jewish News* (Sydney edition)
AJT	*Australian Jewish Times*
HS	*Hebrew Standard of Australasia*
JC	*Jewish Chronicle*
NZJC	*New Zealand Jewish Chronicle*
SJN	*Sydney Jewish News*

Note: In 1987 Melbourne's *Australian Jewish News* and Sydney's *Australian Jewish Times* merged. In 1990 the *Australian Jewish Times* changed its name to *Australian Jewish News* (Sydney edition) and Melbourne's *Australian Jewish News* became known as *Australian Jewish News* (Melbourne edition).

This book is dedicated to the memory of my father

Sidney Lionel Fihlebon (1923–2006)

Words cannot adequately express my love, respect and appreciation

Acknowledgements

I would like to express my appreciation to all the individuals from numerous libraries, archives, universities, schools, Jewish community centres, newspapers, Holocaust museums and exhibitions, Holocaust survivor organisations, and Jewish Boards of Deputies – more than I can list – who contributed towards making this book possible.

I am extremely grateful to George and Hanka Pressburg in Wellington, Phil and Viv Josephs in Auckland, Betty and George Lenham in Sydney, Frances Prince and family in Melbourne, and of course Mum and Dad (Sidney and Rita Fihlebon) in London, for sustaining me with warmth and hospitality during my research trips.

During the writing of this book I was the fortunate recipient of a University of Western Australia (UWA) Postdoctoral Research Fellowship. I would like to thank Dr Sue Broomhall in the History Department, for her friendship and critical feedback on drafts of these chapters, as well as Trudi McGlade in Research Services for her counsel and cheerful, helpful nature. I am grateful also to Professor Konrad Kweit, Professor Yehuda Bauer and Ben Helfgott for giving freely of their time and for sharing their views and feelings about Holocaust remembrance. My utmost appreciation goes to Professor Bill Rubinstein for his insightful comments, sound advice and continued support for my research. An earlier version of chapter five appeared in the *Journal of Modern Jewish Studies* – thanks to Glenda Abramson for her interest and editorial suggestions.

Working with Mark Anstee at Valentine Mitchell has been a pleasure, not only due to his editorial vigilance but for his sympathy and understanding as Dad's illness meant that timelines had to become flexible.

My gratitude also to a far-flung network of friends, including Bette Caley, Orit Rose, Glynis and David Steed, Paul and Jacqui Freedman, Margaret and Graham Robinson, Joanna Sassoon, Kristi Burke and Don Negri, Sue Sadot, Debbie and Stephanie Guz, and Erez Berman. As always thanks to my daughters Ye'elah and Tal, who are an enormous source of happiness and pride. And finally, thanks to my partner, Ian McArthur, without whose love and encouragement this project would not have come to fruition.

Foreword

It is a pleasure and an honour to be asked to write the Foreword to Judith Berman's interesting and important book, *Holocaust Agendas, Conspiracies and Industries?* The memorialization of the Holocaust among the world's Jewish communities has become a ubiquitous feature of contemporary Jewish life, yet, as Dr Berman demonstrates in great detail, it has also been a continuing source of division, dissension and controversy. As she points out, while Holocaust commemorations are today universal throughout the Jewish world, they emerged surprisingly late, and there was often great reluctance to hold such memorial events until the 1970s or even later. In Britain and possibly elsewhere throughout the Commonwealth, this reluctance arose in part from a sense of embarrassment – no other word will do – at what Hitler had managed to do to Europe's Jews, and in part because Jews were very reluctant to claim any entitlement to special moral superiority or recognition in countries whose whole population had suffered grievously during the Second World War. Only after the events of the war passed from the active memory of most inhabitants, becoming a part of history which could be judged objectively, did this reluctance to memorialize the Holocaust pass from Diaspora Jewry, assisted by a new sense of self-confidence engendered by the success of the State of Israel and the discrediting of anti-Semitism. Indeed, this former reluctance has been replaced by something like its precise opposite, a near-ubiquitous obsession with the Holocaust as the central defining event and touchstone of modern Jewish history. This obsession with the Holocaust is also evident among non-Jews, for instance in the academic interests of secondary and tertiary students, for whom the unbelievable evils of the Holocaust are regularly central and seminal. One important reason for the controversies now surrounding the memorialization of the Holocaust is that virtually every group wants to procure its share, as it were, of the moral credibility which has undoubtedly come to the Jews in recent decades for being victims of the greatest crime in history. Albert Camus allegedly told Elie Wiesel that he envied the Jews the Holocaust, by which he presumably meant that it gave to the Jews a special and unique moral credibility as victims which no other group could claim – certainly not, it would seem, the French, with their very mixed record under Vichy.

As Dr Berman also perceptively notes, while the memorialization of the Holocaust should have functioned as possibly the prime force acting to unify the contemporary Jewish world, it has often had precisely the opposite effect, serving, sometimes notoriously, to divide Orthodox and non-Orthodox Jews, and to divide those who wish Holocaust commemoration to be exclusively concerned with the Jewish victims of the Nazis, and those who wish to broaden or indeed universalize its scope. At the present time in Britain, and possibly elsewhere, Muslim groups are at the forefront of those who boycott Holocaust Memorial Day because it commemorates only Jews in the Holocaust. Many wish it specifically to commemorate as well the alleged Palestinian victims of Israeli policy. Most Jews of course regard any such widening of the scope of Holocaust commemoration, let alone to appease groups which are specifically anti-Jewish, as intolerable. Unfortunately, as Western Muslim populations come to dwarf the size of the Diaspora's Jewish communities, and as the Western left bizarrely embraces its seeming polar opposite, fundamentalist Islam, with ever-greater fervour, such demands are likely to grow and perhaps become successful. I am personally one of those who believe that it was a mistake to have enacted a national Holocaust Memorial Day, as Britain has done, precisely because it provides an opportunity for every group, including those who cannot be described as friendly to the Jews, fundamentally to alter a commemoration of Hitler's Jewish victims.

Dr Berman's work, with its comparative description of a number of Western societies, constitutes an important historical insight into how those who have come after the *Shoah* have attempted to understand its incomprehensibility. Precisely because these events are incomprehensible, it has not been surprising that their commemoration has been confused and controversial, and her book will help us to make sense of our halting attempts to make sense of them and mourn their victims.

Professor William D. Rubinstein
University of Wales, Aberystwyth
February 2006

1

Introduction

With the flow of time, events of the past usually recede from public consciousness. This has not been the case with the Holocaust. Despite the passage of more than fifty years, interest in the Holocaust is now at an all time high. There were more front-page stories in the *New York Times* relating to the Holocaust in the first six months of the twenty-first century than during the entire twelve years of the Third Reich.[1] In 2000 there were no fewer than 1,002 university courses on the Holocaust in the United States, taught at 324 different institutions.[2] This year we have seen many European countries observe Holocaust Memorial Day – on 27 January, the date of the liberation of Auschwitz. In Britain, the inaugural Holocaust Memorial Day ceremony at Westminster's Central Hall, attended by Prince Charles and the leaders of Britain's three main political parties, was televised live to approximately 1.5 million viewers. People across Europe and Western civilization have begun increasingly to perceive the Holocaust as a watershed event in the history of humankind, a defining event of the twentieth century, and one that could only be ignored at their peril.

Although systematic historical research about the Holocaust began after the 1961 Eichmann Trial, it is only in the past decade that scholars have turned their attention to the topic of how post-Second World War societies have remembered the Holocaust. A survey of the international Holocaust remembrance literature reveals an increased scholarly interest in Holocaust Day (*Yom haShoah*) commemorations and Holocaust museums. A number of works have analysed the history of the establishment of Holocaust memorials, and representations of the Holocaust in museums.[3] Probably the most significant contribution to this burgeoning literature is James Young's extensive study of selected Holocaust museums and monuments in Poland, Austria, Germany, Israel and the United States, which established that different nations and communities remember the Holocaust selectively according to their past experiences and current lives.[4] Edward T. Linenthal's *Preserving Memory* vividly and sensitively portrayed the debates and pressures that arose at every stage of the creation of the US Holocaust Memorial Museum, from conception to construction and selection of exhibits.[5] Scholars have explored selected aspects of *Yom haShoah* commemorations, usually in Israel or the US. Yael Zerubavel demonstrated how public commemoration of the Holocaust has passed through significant transformations in the Jewish state, while James Young focused on the history and public performance of *Yom haShoah* ceremonies.[6] Rabbi Irving Greenberg examined the rituals and symbols of the services in North America;[7] and Michael Berenbaum discussed the process by which *Yom haShoah* commemorations came to be complemented by 'National Days of Remembrance' in the US.[8] However, in common with most other researchers of Holocaust memorialization, Berenbaum did not extend his analysis to include either the focus of *Yom haShoah* commemorations, or the meanings of the Holocaust that have been conveyed.[9] The time is thus ripe for this detailed analysis of what Jews have learned from the tragedy of the Holocaust.

In contrast to the oft-disregarded 'lessons' of the Holocaust, issues surrounding its 'Americanization' are at the forefront of the Holocaust remembrance literature.[10] Two related matters that have generated considerable discussion have been the politicization and exploitation of Holocaust memory, and the question whether the Holocaust was unique or universal.[11] Michael Berenbaum argued that, as part of the process of making the US Holocaust Memorial Museum relevant to non-Jewish Americans, the Holocaust became 'Americanized', that is, reshaped to reinforce professed American principles and values such as tolerance, democracy, pluralism and human rights.[12] However, Berenbaum maintained that the 'Americanization' of the Holocaust, which was perhaps inevitable in a national institution, did not require its 'dejudaization' – the story of the Holocaust could still remain faithful to the unique historical event.[13] Alvin Rosenfeld has been particularly critical of what he perceived as distortions introduced by the 'Americanization' of the Holocaust.[14] Pointing to the tensions between Jewish and public memory of the Holocaust, Rosenfeld argues that:

> it is essential to acknowledge the difficulties inherent in any attempt to align collective, or public, memory with private Jewish memory. The two are by no means synonymous and, in the end, may not be reconcilable, for behind each are cultural impulses and inclinations that are divergent and perhaps, in their essence, antithetical.[15]

Rosenfeld feared that ultimately Jewish memory would not predominate as public memory in pluralistic North American culture and that, consequently, the centrality and uniqueness of Jewish victimization under Nazism would be diminished.[16] How have these debates been played out in other Jewish Diaspora communities? Has the Holocaust been 'Australianized', 'Anglicized' or 'Kiwized', and, if so, have the universal dimensions of the Holocaust led to the relativization of its uniqueness or to inappropriate misuses and abuses of Holocaust imagery and terminology? Do tensions exist between interpretations of the Holocaust in Jewish and general cultures in Australia, Britain and New Zealand?

Over the past decade, increased academic attention has been focused on post-war responses to the Holocaust with scholars asking how and why that event has moved from the margins of public consciousness to occupy a central place in Western discourse and culture. Perhaps the most stimulating of these academic contributions has been Peter Novick's *The Holocaust in American Life* which charts the history of the American post-war response to the Holocaust, and asks how and why that event has moved from the margins of American Jewish consciousness to occupy a central place in general American discourse.[17] Novick asserts that memory of the Holocaust was utilized by the 'American Jewish leadership' to mobilize support according to shifting Jewish community concerns. In a similar vein, Tim Cole examines three of the Holocaust's most emblematic figures and three of the Holocaust's most visited sites to show us that '*Shoah* business is big business'.[18] Norman Finkelstein's emphasis on the American Jewish leaderships' alleged manipulation of Holocaust memory goes one step further than Novick and Cole. In *The Holocaust Industry*, Finkelstein declares that not only has Holocaust memory been invoked by power hungry 'American Jewish elites' and organizations to shield Israel and the American Jewish community from legitimate criticism but it has also been exploited to extort billions of dollars from European banks, governments and industries, ostensibly as compensation for needy Holocaust survivors but in fact for a range of personal, political and economic ends.[19] These disturbing research findings raise very pertinent questions with regard to the Holocaust remembrance practices of other Diaspora communities. Has Holocaust programming been similarly initiated and 'manipulated' by other Diaspora leaders and organizations to serve a variety of Jewish agendas or were there other factors at play that raised the profile of the Holocaust?

Scholarship that brings these various forms and issues of Holocaust remembrance together is rare and generally focuses on an analysis of Holocaust remembrance in one country. Tom Segev's *The Seventh Million* examines the impact of the Holocaust on the identity, culture and politics of Israel;[20] Tony Kushner's *The Holocaust and the Liberal Imagination* studies the responses and reactions of Britain (and to a lesser extent of the US) to the Holocaust; Franklin Bialystok explores the evolution of the legacy of the Holocaust in the collective memory of the Canadian Jewish community, and this author has examined patterns of Holocaust remembrance in Australia.[21] These researchers have examined various forms and issues of Holocaust remembrance in one country or community but have not addressed the broad comparative aspect. David Wyman examines the impact of the Holocaust on twenty-two countries from 1945 to the mid-1990s.[22] However, analysis of experiences in Australia and New Zealand are excluded and the focus is predominantly on general society; Holocaust remembrance practices in Jewish communities are hardly mentioned. The same can be said with regard to Judith Miller's *One, by One, by One*, which analyses the ways that the Holocaust has been remembered, suppressed, distorted and misused in Germany, the Soviet Union, the US, Austria, Holland and France.[23] James Young's description and critique of selected Holocaust memorials is both extensive and ground-breaking in its approach but memorials in Australia, Britain or New Zealand are not included. Despite these innovative and sophisticated works of scholarship, a significant gap in Holocaust studies persists. There has yet to be a systematic comparative analysis of how 'Jewish people', who were actual or prospective victims of Nazism, have commemorated such an immense tragedy.

This book brings a comparative dimension that is lacking in nearly all scholarly contributions to studies of Holocaust memorialization. Australia, Britain and New Zealand, all significant Diaspora communities, which have either been previously ignored or received little or no attention, will now be incorporated into the international mosaic of scholarship about Holocaust remembrance. This study of Holocaust remembrance practices raises important questions about the impact of such factors as geographical location, the size of a Jewish population and its component of Holocaust survivors, and the nature of the host country, on the ways in which the Holocaust has been remembered. Conclusions that have been based on the experiences of Israeli and North American Jewry should no longer be generalized for the entire Jewish Diaspora. The result will be the emergence of a more nuanced understanding of Holocaust memorialization.

Australia, Britain and New Zealand make for interesting comparisons in relation to Holocaust remembrance. There are both striking similarities as well as major differences in the evolution of these Jewish communities.

While Australian, British and New Zealand Jewry developed under the same flag, speaking the same language and with similar political systems, they are divided by geography. Britain is located close to both the killing fields of the Holocaust and the post-war centres of world Jewry (Israel and the US), while Australia and New Zealand, thousands of miles away from the West but attached to it in so many ways, have often been considered as 'frontier societies', or as being on 'the edge of the Diaspora'.[24] This study examines whether each community's geographical location has influenced the ways in which the Holocaust has been remembered.

An analysis of Jewish population in general, and Holocaust survivor population in particular, reveals significant differences between the three Jewish communities. At the turn of the millennium, Anglo Jewry numbered around 346,000, Australia about 110,000, and New Zealand about 8,000.[25] Not only do the sizes of the communities contrast, but also their composition. The Jewish population of Australia, which was 26,472 in 1933,[26] more than doubled as a result of the migration between 1933 and 1963 of about 35–40,000 Jews, who either had left Europe to escape Nazism or were survivors of the Holocaust.[27] Post-war Melbourne may have proportionately the highest percentage of Holocaust survivors of any Diaspora Jewish community.[28] The pre- and post-war migrants changed not only the size of the Australian Jewish community, but also its nature. Colin Golvan, a Melbourne author and broadcaster, paints a very dismal picture of Australian Jewry prior to the arrival of the European refugees and survivors:

> But for the war, Jewish life in Australia would have languished. It is one of the ironies of the Holocaust that for all its tragic circumstances, the survivors gave new hope to Jewish outposts which were dying out, not through extermination but sheer inconsequentiality.[29]

The overwhelming majority of these mainly Central and East European Jewish immigrants settled in Melbourne and Sydney and were instrumental in invigorating existing, and establishing new, Jewish community institutions which would foster Jewish survival in the aftermath of the Holocaust.[30]

In 1933 Anglo-Jewry was the seventh or eighth largest Jewish community in the world, with a population of about 300,000. In 1945 it had become the second or third largest Jewish community in Europe and the fourth or fifth largest community in the Diaspora.[31] Anglo-Jewry, with the exception of the Channel Islands, survived the Holocaust intact and increased in size as a result of pre- and post-war Jewish immigration.

During the 1930s over 60,000 Jewish refugees from Nazism had been admitted to Britain, including 9,739 children through the *Kinderstransporte* scheme. Post-war Jewish immigration to Britain was limited. Just over 700 children arrived on the Children from the Concentration Camp scheme, another one or two thousand Holocaust survivors via the Distressed Relatives Scheme and perhaps another thousand or so from Hungary and Poland in the 1950s and 1960s.[32] New Zealand Jewry also comprises only a small percentage of Holocaust survivors. Only about 1,300 Jews were permitted to enter New Zealand between 1933 and 1942 when the government's immigration policy was restrictive against racial minorities. After 1945 discrimination continued against those, including Jews, considered unsuitable on racial, national and economic grounds. This book considers the impact of Holocaust refugees and survivors on patterns of Holocaust memorialization in Australia, Britain and New Zealand.

How have the changing attitudes towards minorities in Australia, Britain and New Zealand affected Holocaust memorialization? For the first three decades after the Holocaust both Anglo and New Zealand Jewry continued their pre-war trend of adopting a low profile, scared of pressing particularistic claims for fear of antagonizing the gentile community and arousing anti-Semitism. The prevailing monocultural assimilationist frameworks of British and New Zealand society worked against expressions of difference.[33] Australian Jewry was also somewhat limited by Australian government policies of assimilation and integration of minorities, but felt more confident to assert particularistic concerns to general society when deemed necessary.[34] From the early 1970s Australian government policy increasingly replaced assimilation and integration of minorities with 'multiculturalism', on the assumption that the varied ethnic traditions of migrants would enrich Australian society.[35] It was to take at least a decade after multiculturalism had been introduced to Australia that Britain started moving towards a more pluralistic society, one which provided space for ethnic, religious and other groups to identify and express themselves openly. New Zealand, which since the Maori renaissance of the 1980s has recognized itself as bicultural (composed of those of Maori and European [Pakeha] descent), has only recently begun to struggle with the concept of multiculturalism – which would include consideration of the cultural concerns and interests of increasingly multi-ethnic New Zealand society.[36] This study focuses attention on the link between Holocaust memorialization and moves towards increased pluralism in Australia, Britain and New Zealand.

Ironically, the relatively low level of anti-Semitism and the high degree of tolerance in increasingly pluralistic Australia, Britain and New Zealand have given rise to intermarriage and assimilation; sometimes inappropriately referred to as the 'silent Holocaust'. Anglo-Jewry is decreasing in size. Despite the pre- and post-war Jewish immigration to Britain, Anglo-Jewry declined from a peak of about 390,000 in the early to mid-1950s to about 346,000 in 2001.[37] Significant increases in inter-marriage and assimilation have been one of the major reasons cited for Anglo-Jewry's community's demographic fall off. About only a third of Jews of marriageable age in Britain are marrying in synagogues.[38] Australian Jewry shares these concerns about assimilation but, largely as a result of migration from South Africa and the former Soviet Union, has been steadily increasing in size. New Zealand Jewry's demography – small, dispersed and isolated from the main Jewish centres – has caused many to migrate to the vibrant communities of Melbourne and Sydney.[39] Indeed, the relationship between Australian and New Zealand Jewry has been neatly summed up by Beaglehole and Levine, who conclude that 'the private, low-key nature of contemporary Kiwi Jewishness looks a lot like the pre-war Australian communities', that is, ripe for assimilation.[40] This book considers how these divergent population trends will impact on the future evolution of Holocaust memorialization.

High intermarriage rates and assimilation are not the only concerns shared by Australian, British and New Zealand Jewry. The trauma of the Holocaust, articulated or not, is borne by Jews worldwide. Neo-Nazism, Holocaust denial and the emergence of far left-wing anti-Zionism have further added to Jewish insecurities. These threats to Jewish physical and spiritual continuity, which have become central to the Jewish psyche, have determined that Jewish survival predominates on the communal agenda. Common Jewish responses to the threats from anti-Semitism, anti-Zionism, neo-Nazism and assimilation have been to increase efforts in Jewish education, to reinforce Jewish commitment, and to urge support for Israel.

This books seeks to elucidate and explain the significance of these similarities and differences for evolving patterns of Holocaust remembrance in Australia, Britain and New Zealand. I ask whether parallel Holocaust remembrance patterns have evolved or whether unique political, social and cultural developments in each country, and varia-tions in Jewish community size and composition, have led to diverse trends in Holocaust memorialization. Moreover, I explore whether the processes of Holocaust memorialization in these Diaspora communities reveal different trends from the American experience. In these ways an important gap in the field of comparative Holocaust remembrance studies will be filled.

At this point it is pertinent to point out that there has been no single, united, post-war Jewish 'community' in Australia, Britain or New Zealand, but rather, a variety of different, sometimes antagonistic, sometimes overlapping 'communities', including religious, regional, socio-economic and ideological.[41] Jewish 'community' is an elusive concept that defies definition. For the readers of this book it should be understood as including anyone who perceives him or herself as belonging to any one or more of these 'communities'.

Two main strategies have been adopted to examine the complex relationship between a particular Jewish community's Holocaust remembrance practices, the past experiences, current realities and self-understandings of that community, and the dominant cultures in the country of which the community forms a part. Firstly, this study uses a rich and varied collection of source material. The project has generated and evaluated some new primary sources while other primary sources have been used for the first time. The main primary source material is the Jewish press, including the *New Zealand Jewish Chronicle (NZJC)*,[42] Britain's *Jewish Chronicle (JC)*,[43] and *Australian Jewish News (AJN)*. These Jewish newspaper sources, which include reports, photographs, articles, letters and editorials, are complemented by references to the Holocaust in the mainstream national press and media. Newspaper sources have been supplemented by various archival materials including the Minutes and Annual Reports of the *Yom haShoah* and Holocaust museum and monument planning committees, observation of Holocaust remembrance activities, catalogues of Holocaust museums and exhibitions (or when unavailable a complete set of the written text and photograph captions), museum newsletters, survivor association newsletters, and oral history interviews with survivors and their descendants as well as other members of the Jewish community who have been involved in Holocaust remembrance activities.

The second strategy to be adopted in this book is an examination of how key historiographical and cultural debates, which cut across the various public forms of Holocaust remembrance, have been played out in Australia, Britain and New Zealand. Original questions are raised, some of the assumptions that have underpinned existing studies have been reanalysed, and exciting new ways of thinking about Holocaust remembrance are introduced.

The politics of memory informs my research. French theorist Michel Foucault has deepened our awareness of the use of memory as a resource in the mobilization of social and political power.[44] Chapter two, which acknowledges the politics of memory, is concerned with the processes by which the Holocaust entered Jewish and mainstream cultures in Australia, Britain and New Zealand. It examines how decisions have been arrived at in the field of Holocaust memorialization, paying particular attention to the roles of Jewish leadership elites and Holocaust survivors. Did Jewish organizations initiate and promote Holocaust remembrance or were other factors at play that explain the current high level of Holocaust awareness in the societies under analysis? This chapter reveals some very different trends from the American experience as presented by Novick.

Chapter three examines how debates over the uniqueness and universality of the Holocaust have been reflected in representations of the Holocaust and its meanings at *Yom haShoah* commemorations and Holocaust museums and exhibitions in Australia, Britain and New Zealand. Whereas scholarly research has previously focused on the process by which the Holocaust has entered the consciousness of general society, this chapter concentrates on whether Jewish social memory of the Holocaust has changed through the process of sharing that memory with society. Also considered, is the extent to which socio-cultural and political histories of the countries in which the remembering is taking place have impacted on the formulation of representations of the Holocaust and their meanings.[45] Thus this chapter relates to the boundaries of Holocaust remembrance − who and what is remembered or strategically forgotten, and to what ends? Have representations of the Holocaust focused on the unique fate of the Jewish victims of the Holocaust? Have a plurality of experiences of the Holocaust been conveyed, or have certain memories been annihilated? Have *Yom haShoah* commemorations and Holocaust museums and exhibitions conveyed only the Jewish or also universal humanistic lessons of the Holocaust?

Chapter four examines how the terminology and imagery of the Holocaust have been casually, and ever more frequently, used and evoked by those wishing to attract a larger audience to their cause; be it for financial, emotional or political gain. This chapter argues that we bear a responsibility to the victims and survivors of those horrific events, as well as to the 'historical truth', to critique, evaluate, respond to and talk about what is acceptable usage and what is not. Examining a variety of invocations of the Holocaust and its imagery, from the general media as well as from Jewish sources, this chapter suggests the adoption of historical accuracy as a criterion for distinguishing between appropriate and inappropriate uses of the Holocaust. While comparisons between the Holocaust and other events either before or since are welcomed, they must be expressed responsibly and ethically, which means that differences as well as similarities must be rigorously elucidated. Comparisons are inappropriate if they focus only on isolated characteristics of complex experiences and events. Historical accuracy must be adopted, both by Jews and non-Jews, as a standard for good practice.

Chapter five, which conceptualizes collective memory as a contested terrain, is informed by social memory theory. This study incorporates what French sociologist Maurice Halbwachs has called 'collective memory'. Writing in the 1920s, Halbwachs observed that memory is socially constructed, dynamic and connected to group and national identities which change over time.[46] Our understanding of the relationships between memory, nationalism and identity has been furthered by Eric Hobsbawm's notions of 'invented traditions' and 'usable pasts', and Benedict Anderson's 'imagined communities'.[47] Selected episodes of Holocaust memorialization shed light on the tense and ambiguous relationship between Holocaust remembrance and Jewish unity. Many have shared the aspiration for Jewish unity at Holocaust remembrance functions but, as these case studies demonstrate, despite the high level of cohesion achieved by the atmosphere of collective mourning, they have also been occasions of conflict and disunity.

Chapter six enters into new areas of scholarship as it explores whether past experiences of suffering and trauma, personal or vicarious, have led to greater sensitivity and compassion towards the tragedies and traumas of others. This case study identifies that Holocaust survivors and their descendants have been increasingly applying their actual or vicarious memories of the Holocaust to Australian social and political contexts. These understandings of the universal humanistic lessons of the Holocaust are in turn impacting on the wider Jewish community, bringing about broader Australian Jewish engagement with human rights and social justice issues in Australia.

This study of the ways in which the Holocaust has been remembered in Australia, Britain and New Zealand problematizes the understandings of Holocaust memorialization that have emerged from focusing predominantly on the Israeli and North American experiences. This in turn contributes to a more nuanced and richer appreciation of the experiences of Diaspora Jewry.

2

Memorializing the Holocaust: A Hidden Agenda?

It is generally agreed upon among historians that feelings of vulnerability and isolation which accompanied Israel's 1967 Six Day War, and the real danger of annihilation during the first days of the 1973 Yom Kippur War, increased Jewish awareness of, and interest in, the Holocaust.[1] However, Peter Novick dismisses this interpretation as too simplistic. He asserts that there was a 'massive investment by Jewish communal organizations in promoting "Holocaust consciousness"'.[2] 'Holocaust programming' was allegedly initiated and 'manipulated' according to shifting Jewish community concerns – to deflect criticism from Israel, to provide a usable past to unite American Jewry in the present, and to foster Jewish identity which, it was hoped, would serve as a barrier to the rising tide of intermarriage and assimilation. Novick's thrust is that the current high level of Holocaust awareness in American Jewish life did not arrive spontaneously but was calculated by Jewish organizations and leaders to serve a variety of Jewish agendas. The implication is that without the promotion of the Holocaust by the American Jewish organizations, Zionists and conservatives, the Holocaust would not have become so central to American Jewish identity and general American culture.[3]

Novick's disturbing research findings raise very pertinent questions with regard to the Holocaust remembrance practices of other Diaspora communities. Has Holocaust programming been similarly initiated and 'manipulated' by Jewish leaders and organizations to serve a variety of Jewish agendas or were there other factors at play that raised the profile of the Holocaust? This chapter, which analyses how the Holocaust entered public discourse and became a central component of Jewish culture and identity in Australia, Britain and New Zealand, reveals some very different trends from the American experience as presented by Novick.

As news of the Warsaw Ghetto Uprising reached Diaspora Jewish communities, conscious efforts were made by a range of Jewish organizations to commemorate the heroism of the revolt. This urge to recall and reconstruct the past, which has occurred annually in Jewish communities worldwide, can be explained by the intrinsic power of the event. These memorial functions, which evolved to include not only remembrance of the Warsaw Ghetto Uprising but also of the six million Jewish victims of Nazism, became referred to as *Yom haShoah* (Holocaust Day) commemorations.

In New Zealand, these memorials were low-key affairs. They usually took place immediately after regular synagogue services and thus tended to attract mainly the regular synagogue attendees. In 1961, after another disappointing turn out, Auckland's Rabbi Astor commented:

> It is to be regretted that the attendance at the service was disap-
> pointingly small. Similar services in other parts of the world are
> always attended by large numbers and if there is to be an annual
> commemoration it is to be hoped that a greater number of members
> of the community will attend to pay their respects to the martyrs.[4]

Astor was ill informed with regards to commemorations in other communities. Even in Australia and Britain, where Holocaust memorial functions were held in public halls or Jewish community centres, only a narrow section of the Jewish population – mostly Holocaust survivors from Eastern Europe and their families – were present. Until the 1980s, few Australian or British-born Jews attended.[5]

Jewish leadership elites, both secular and religious, failed to take a leading role in Holocaust memorialization. The Orthodox establishment perceived Holocaust commemorations as inappropriate, arguing that Holocaust remembrance should be integrated into the religious calendar and commemorated in synagogues and the home. The roots of this approach are found in debates in Israel where the rabbinical authorities had designated the Fast of Tevet on 10 Tevet, and not the 27 Nisan as selected by the Knesset, as the Remembrance Day for Jewish martyrs and heroes of the Holocaust.[6] The Orthodox Rabbinical leadership in Australia and Britain rarely issued announcements or directives to ministers in connection with the day of mourning fixed by the Knesset.[7] Rabbis tended to attend when invited to officiate; otherwise they were conspicuous by their absence.[8] In 1963 the United Synagogue, Britain's largest Orthodox congregation, even rejected the suggestion of the principal organizers of the annual memorial evening to mark the occasion of the twentieth anniversary of the Warsaw ghetto uprising by placing a Holocaust commemorative plaque on their property. The

United Synagogue felt that the main entrance hall of their head office at Woburn House 'would not be the appropriate place' and suggested one of their cemeteries instead.[9]

Australian Jewry, comprising a high percentage of refugees from Nazism and Holocaust survivors and their descendants, has been more aware of the Holocaust than many other Diaspora communities. Yet, for almost three decades after liberation, each state's Board of Deputies (the umbrella organization of Jewish organizations in each state) limited itself to assisting in the organization of the annual *Yom haShoah* commemorations and supporting the establishment of Holocaust monuments at Carlton and Rookwood cemeteries in 1963 and 1970 respectfully.[10] Yet, in comparison to their counterpart in Britain, the Boards of Deputies of the various Australian states were supportive of Holocaust remembrance. For thirty years following the end of the Second World War the Board of Deputies of British Jews (BODOBJ) was largely inactive and unconcerned in respect to Holocaust memorialization.[11] Only from 1961 did the Board of Deputies of British Jews officially participate in the annual memorial function in London and, unless invited to speak, deputies of the Board rarely attended.[12] Throughout the 1960s and much of the 1970s, the Board of Deputies of British Jews responded half-heartedly to efforts of other organizations to establish a permanent Holocaust memorial.[13] Whereas the predominantly Australian or British born Jewish community leaders in Melbourne and Sydney had lent their support for the establishment of Holocaust monuments at Carlton and Rookwood cemeteries, in 1960 the Board of Deputies of British Jews responded to initiatives for a permanent Holocaust memorial with the recommendation that 'an appropriate Memorial would be the placing of a permanent light in a suitable part of synagogues, and the suggestion was adopted that all Deputies should invite their synagogues to adopt this method where practicable'.[14] Holocaust survivors and others in the community must have wondered under what circumstances this suggestion would not be practicable. In 1961 the Board provided modest financial support for a survivor-initiated exhibition about the Warsaw Ghetto Uprising[15] but it did not consider this as 'essential work'.[16]

Any attempt to explain the Board of Deputies of British Jews' half-hearted approach to Holocaust memorialization during these years cannot ignore Britain's narrative of the Second World War. The myth that Britain 'stood alone' to defeat Nazism did not provide space for the remembrance of other, perhaps greater suffering. As long as there were direct memories of British war experiences, those of the Holocaust would be overshadowed. Indeed, this was probably not at odds with the understandings of many Anglo-Jews who perceived their suffering in the Second World War in common with their non-Jewish neighbours.[17]

It must be pointed out that Britain is not such an exception. The political and social climates in other 'free world', post-war societies did not encourage Holocaust memorialization. Most gentiles and Jews, whether due to guilt that they had not done more to help, or embarrassment over the perception that the Jews had gone 'like sheep to the slaughter', wanted to forget the horrors and sufferings of the past and instead focus on the future. Consequently, survivors, many of who felt a need to bear witness for those who had perished under Nazism, received little encouragement to tell their stories. For about thirty years following the Second World War many and perhaps most survivors repressed their painful memories of the Holocaust and concentrated instead on their physical, psychological and emotional recovery.

Yet perhaps the most significant factor contributing to the dearth of Holocaust memorialization in the first three post-war decades was the lack of support for ethnicity, or for minority groups in the countries of the Jewish Diaspora. In Britain, the basic premise of the prevailing monocultural liberal assimilationist ideology worked against expressions of difference.[18] Scared of arousing anti-Semitism at home, Anglo Jewish leadership elites refrained from drawing attention to any particularist concerns, including Holocaust remembrance. A similar situation prevailed in monocultural New Zealand and Australia.

Three decades were to pass before the Holocaust became a major component of Jewish culture and identity. Awareness of the Holocaust was temporarily raised by post-war Holocaust-related events, such as the rehabilitation and rearmament of West Germany,[19] the subject of material reparations from West Germany, and the 1961 Eichmann Trial.[20] The impact of Israel's 1967 Six Day War and the 1973 Yom Kippur War on Diaspora Jewry cannot be overestimated. Diaspora Jewry was fearful for the fate of the State of Israel. Peter Wertheim, a child of Holocaust survivors who settled in Sydney, recalled that the shadow of the Holocaust emerged from his subconscious in the weeks leading up to the Six Day War:

> the Jewish people, and particularly for *Shoah* survivors and their descendants ... remember the excruciating anxiety which the entire Jewish world felt in the days leading up to the war, when Egypt's flagrant acts of belligerency against Israel were accompanied by its leader's boast that he would wipe Israel off the map, and Arab mobs throughout the Middle East were shown on television baying for

Jewish blood. For many *Shoah* survivors it was a bit like waking up from a nightmare only to find that the nightmare was actually happening. Even if the *Shoah* was not openly talked about in the anxious days leading up to the 1967 war, its memory hung like an ominous cloud over the entire Jewish people.[21]

Melbourne Jewry, especially those born in Eastern Europe in Yiddish-speaking homes who had suffered under the Nazis,[22] were deeply absorbed in the 1967 Middle East crisis. British Jewry was also deeply affected by the Six Day War. Chief Rabbi Sir Jonathan Sacks observed that after the war Jews finally discovered the Holocaust: 'It was as if it took the threat of a second devastation to unlock the floodgates of feeling about the first'.[23] Peter Novick's contention that the 'American Jewish leadership' promoted the Holocaust to the centre of American Jewish identity and public discourse after Israel's policies in the 1980s and 1990s increasingly divided North American Jewry and discounts the deep trauma experienced by Diaspora Jewry before the Six Day War and during the first few days of the Yom Kippur War. Perhaps Novick disregarded the significance of this factor on raising awareness of the Holocaust because changes in Holocaust memorialization did not result immediately.

Indeed, the annual *Yom haShoah* commemorations remained almost the only public form of Holocaust remembrance until the late 1970s, when a number of interrelated processes, including a range of representations of the Holocaust and Holocaust-related events and issues, further stimulated and intensified interest in the destruction of European Jewry. A significant stimulus to Holocaust awareness in Diaspora communities was the 1978 screening of the US-made mini series *Holocaust*, based on a novel by Gerald Green. The televised dramatization was the top rated TV programme in Australia in 1978, viewed by just under half of the population.[24] In Britain, 19 million watched the final two episodes.[25] Holocaust survivor, Marla Tribich, stated 'This has brought it into the open, made people think and jogged their memories'.[26] Towards the screening, the *New Zealand Listener* included a four-page article based on interviews with Holocaust survivors who told their stories, some for the first time in detail, in response to attempts to deny the Holocaust. One New Zealander, who agreed to be identified only by 73660, her concentration camp number, recognized the appeal of *Holocaust* to wider New Zealand society: 'I think it's a good idea to show it because I feel people don't always want to see a documentary. This [film] involves a family, maybe it's nearer to human beings.'[27] Discussions surrounding *Holocaust* in the mainstream and Jewish press brought the subject closer to the consciousness of the Jewish and wider populations in Australia, Britain and New Zealand.

Increased interest in the Holocaust was sustained by the publication of numerous books on various aspects of the Holocaust, the continuing debates about the possibility of prosecuting Nazi war criminals, the furore surrounding US President Ronald Reagan's 1985 visit to Bitburg (perceived in the Jewish world as an attempt to forget the crimes of Nazism), the Waldheim affair, the imbroglio over the Carmelite convent at Auschwitz, the 1993 opening of the US Holocaust Memorial Museum in Washington DC, and the Barbie and Demjanjuk trials. Stephen Spielberg's *Schindler's List* (based on *Schindler's Ark*), perhaps more than any other single factor, thrust the Holocaust into the international arena. The 1994 movie aroused widespread discussion in Jewish communities and beyond. Sam Lipski, editor-in-chief of the *Australian Jewish News*, referred to it as 'the longest-running controversy, certainly the most emotionally arousing, this paper has featured in recent years... we published 11 articles and columns, each ranging in length from 700 to 1700 words, 26 letters to the editor, and one editorial'.[28]

In this climate of interest in the Holocaust, survivors became increasingly more willing to recall their memories publicly. Many survivors were approaching retirement and had time to reflect on their lives; some were compelled by a feeling of urgency to bear witness as they approached old age. The increased organization and assertiveness of Holocaust survivors in the US and Israel, in particular the 1981 International Gathering of Jewish Holocaust Survivors in Jerusalem and the 1983 American Gathering, was an additional dynamic influencing many survivors in the Diaspora to break their silence. Arguably, more than any other factor, survivors told their stories in response to Holocaust denial literature which had increased worldwide from the late 1970s. Two main groups deny the existence of the Holocaust. On the one hand, Marxists and leftist Palestinian sympathizers claimed that Zionists collaborated with the Nazis and sacrificed their fellow European Jews for their own political need, to create sympathy for the establishment of the State of Israel.[29] On the extreme right, neo-Nazis claimed that the Holocaust was a Zionist hoax supported by fabricated evidence and invented to gain world sympathy for the establishment of the State of Israel.[30] Holocaust denial literature is an attack on survivors' memories and hence on their identities, and was the catalyst behind the decision of many to speak publicly about their personal experiences of the Holocaust. Jewish community leadership elites may have encouraged, but they did not initiate or 'organize', this development.

Although a variety of interrelated influences led to a raising of Holocaust consciousness in Australia, Britain and New Zealand, institutionalized Holocaust memorialization in each of these countries took a different path. Let us first turn our attention to New Zealand Jewry.

In the 1970s Maori leaders and organizations began resisting pressures to become more Pakeha-like and demanded for a reverse trend in race relations, that is for Pakeha to reciprocate by learning about Maori language and culture. New Zealand's subsequent move towards an ideology of biculturalism in the 1980s provided more space than previous monocultural policies, for ethnic, religious and other minority groups to promote their cultural concerns and issues.[31] In this relatively improved social and cultural climate a number of prominent Jewish community leaders organized a commemorative event in Wellington to mark the fortieth anniversary of the liberation of the death camps.[32] The initiators of this first major public Holocaust remembrance activity in New Zealand were inspired by their desire to make known to the wider community the 'amazing' stories of Holocaust survivors.[33] The success of the event and the subsequent public interest about the Holocaust encouraged Hanka Pressburg to devote time to educate wider New Zealand society about the Holocaust. By 1989 Hanka and her husband George had almost single-handedly created a modest Holocaust exhibition in the Wellington Community Centre's library. Schools, service and church groups visit the exhibition and hear a survivors' story as part of their tour of the Wellington Jewish Community Centre.[34] They are also shown a 'Book of Remembrance' of hundreds of names of relatives of New Zealanders who died in the Holocaust which serves to 'show to all those, who one day might claim "it never happened"'.[35] Despite the relative poverty of the exhibit (Holocaust memorabilia hastily displayed in bookshelves behind glass windows), school-teachers return annually with different groups of students to hear the raw power of personal testimony.[36]

Hanka and George Pressburg were also instrumental in arranging for the 'Children of the Holocaust: Drawings from the Terezin Concentration Camp' exhibition of children's drawings and poems to tour New Zealand from 1996 to 1999. Having secured funding from Fred Turnovsky, a fellow Holocaust survivor, the Pressburgs travelled to loan drawings, paintings, collages and poems from the original exhibition in the Jewish Museum in Prague. They then arranged for framing by a local community member, and organized for the necessary sponsors in each location. The exhibition was held at museums and community centres throughout both islands, and by the end of 1998 had been visited by over 136,000 people. The drawings and paintings of fifty children aged 6–14 from Terezin were accompanied by five poems, background information panels on the Holocaust, and one video about Terezin concentration camp and another about the New Zealand Jewish community. Events and activities with local Jewish communities complemented the exhibition in many locations. 'Children of the Holocaust' was accompanied by a comprehensive curriculum-linked education guide, prepared by the Ministry of Education and the Regional Council, which contained background material and other resources. Media interest in daily and community newspapers and radio coverage was widespread and 'Children of the Holocaust' became the longest touring exhibition ever in New Zealand.[37] However, over the past decade, as Wellington Jews have moved in their droves to the more vibrant Jewish centres in Auckland, Melbourne and Sydney, those remaining, including the Pressburgs and other ageing survivors, have little energy left beyond their usual contributions to the annual commemorations and the maintenance of the exhibition in the Jewish centre. Holocaust memorialization seems to have run its course in this ageing and dwindling Jewish community.

For over forty years, the poorly attended annual commemorations were almost the only public form of Holocaust remembrance in Auckland.[38] In the early 1990s Ruth and Sol Filler, the latter a Holocaust survivor, decided that it was time that Auckland had a memorial to the Holocaust and to that end, with a small group of likeminded people, established the Holocaust Memorial Committee. The first of three projects undertaken by the committee was a Holocaust sculpture, which was unveiled at the fiftieth anniversary of the Warsaw Ghetto Uprising in 1993, a high profile public event which attracted an audience of 600 Jews and non-Jews. The following year, brass commemorative plaques, inscribed with the names of over 1,000 relatives of Auckland Jews who were murdered in the Holocaust, were consecrated in a moving ceremony attended by about 250 in the Auckland Hebrew Community Centre. Part three of the Holocaust remembrance project was the placing of a memorial stone at Auckland's Jewish cemetery in Waikumete.[39] Also in the 1990s, an Oral History Group, comprising mainly of Holocaust survivors and their children, was established to collect oral histories and documentation from survivors who had escaped Nazi persecution.[40] The group's founder and coordinator, Freda Narev, stated that the publicity in the press and on talk-back radio surrounding the imminent visit of Holocaust denier, David Irving, to New Zealand, was a major motivating force behind the group's activities: 'Our main aim was to gather evidence against revisionism'.[41]

With the exception of the 1993 commemoration, public forms of Holocaust remembrance in Auckland, including the sculpture, plaques and memorial stone, have been located in Jewish, not public, space and have focused on educating New Zealand Jewry about the Holocaust. In contrast, the first permanent exhibition about the Holocaust, established at the Auckland War Memorial Museum in 1997, was aimed at educating wider New Zealand society about the events that overcame European Jewry between 1933 and 1945.[42] The exhibition, initiated by the Filler family and funded mainly by Holocaust survivors, was designed by museum staff as part of the Remembering New Zealanders at War, *Scars on the Heart*, permanent exhibition. Set in a darkened alcove, the exhibition opens with an overview of the Holocaust before documenting the personal stories of survival of a number of Auckland survivors.

The main initiators of Holocaust memorialization have been Holocaust survivors and their families. They established modest Holocaust exhibitions and monuments with the aim that memory of the Holocaust would be perpetuated for future generations. New Zealand Jewish leadership elites, in the main descended from Anglo-Jews from the mid-1800s or Eastern Europeans from the 1880s, responded to the initiatives of survivors; they did not lead Holocaust memorialization in any meaningful way.[43] Many of those whose families had not been directly affected by Nazi persecution were detached from the Holocaust; others felt uncomfortable drawing attention to their ethnicity, for example, by organizing a Holocaust exhibition, for fear that it would draw attention to Jews and provoke anti-Semitism.[44] The persistence of such perceptions in New Zealand today reflects Jewish discomfort in further raising Holocaust memorialization in a market saturated with issues pertaining to Maoridom.[45] Ironically, outbursts of Holocaust denial may be a factor in changing New Zealand Jewish attitudes towards public remembrance of the Holocaust. The New Zealand Jewish Council (NZJCO), an umbrella organization of Jewish regional councils, publicly confronted Canterbury University's award of an MA to Joel Hayward for his 1993 Holocaust denial thesis.[46] The NZJCO's active role in fighting the Haywood and the more recent Kupka Holocaust denial case suggests that fear of Holocaust denial could direct New Zealand Jewish elites to take more of a leadership role in supporting survivors' efforts to memorialize the Holocaust.[47]

Holocaust survivors played a central role in establishing public forms of Holocaust remembrance in Australia too. However, two factors, largely absent in New Zealand, have aided Holocaust survivors in Australia to achieve their goal of perpetuating memories of the Holocaust. Firstly, they comprised a significant proportion of Australian Jewry and by the 1980s their voices were being clearly heard, not only in survivor, but also in mainstream, Jewish organizations. Secondly, and perhaps more significantly, changes, more far reaching than those over the Tasman, were taking place in the nature of Australian society and culture. From the early 1970s Australian government policies increasingly replaced assimilation and integration of minorities with 'multiculturalism', on the assumption that the varied ethnic traditions of migrants would enrich Australian society.[48] Australian Jewish historian Suzanne Rutland explains that this change 'has allowed Jews to feel that they can live more authentically as Jews than did the Anglo-Jews of the pre-1945 era'.[49] Living authentically as Jews included memorializing the Holocaust.

In 1980 Melbourne Jewry staged a Holocaust Exhibition which, at that time, was the first, largest and most comprehensive single exhibition devoted to the Holocaust ever staged in Australia. Organized under the auspices of *B'nai B'rith*[50] in conjunction with the Jewish Museum of Australia, the Holocaust remembrance committee of the Board of Deputies, and a range of Holocaust refugee and survivor organizations,[51] the exhibition was a response to increasing Holocaust denial, which was particularly disturbing to Melbourne Jewry, with its high proportion of Holocaust survivors.[52] An exhibition about the Holocaust, which focused on the events surrounding European Jewry between 1933 and 1945, had been considered a more appropriate response than entering a public debate which could give undue attention to denial literature.[53] Allan Nahum, Chairman of the 1980 Holocaust Exhibition in Melbourne, stated that 'there is universal agreement that the implications of an exhibition of this type, at a time when revisionist historians are calling into doubt the veracity of the Holocaust, cannot be underestimated for the good of the community'.[54]

The perceived success of the 1980 Holocaust Exhibition[55] led the *Kadimah*, the communal and cultural centre for the *Yiddish*-speaking community in Melbourne, and the Australian Federation of Polish Jews, two non-mainstream Jewish community organizations consisting predominantly of pre-war refugees and Holocaust survivors, to push for the establishment of a permanent Holocaust Centre in Melbourne. It was envisaged that such a Centre would gather material about the Holocaust and make it available to the Australian public, as well as serving as a focal point from which to counter Holocaust denial.[56] The first public meeting to discuss a Centre was held in March 1983, and the Jewish Holocaust Museum and Research Centre (JHM&RC), founded by the

Kadimah and the Australian Federation of Polish Jews, under the patronage of *Yad Vashem*, was opened in March 1984.[57] The Museum's initial co-Presidents, Bono Wiener and Aron Sokolowicz, both Holocaust survivors, were the principal inspiration and driving force behind its creation.[58] Both had cherished a dream of preserving the memory of the Holocaust in an educational institution that would teach future generations of Jews and non-Jews about the Nazi attempt to annihilate European Jewry. Photographs and memorabilia, which Wiener and Sokolowicz had collected during and after the Holocaust, became the foundation of the permanent display of the Holocaust Centre.[59]

The Holocaust Centre has been overwhelmingly dependent on Holocaust survivors for its creation, expansion and success.[60] The compulsion to tell the world their stories, and those of victims who did not endure, had kept many survivors alive during the Holocaust. The same incentive inspired survivors to devote hours of their time to work at the museum.[61] Kitia Altman explained why she related her painful past, despite the trauma involved:

> Getting older, we become aware that our voices can't be heard forever. The [David] Irving interview was a turning point for me. I thought to myself, I am still alive and he tells me there was no Auschwitz. A lot of people reacted to that. A lot of survivors rang up the Holocaust Centre, wanting to deposit their memories, where before they couldn't talk about it. Since then I made it my policy to talk at forums when I am asked to.[62]

Holocaust survivors have been the backbone of the museum, working in all aspects of its organization from 'behind the scenes', on various projects or daily maintenance and administrative tasks, to speaking to groups and accompanying them on their tour around the permanent display of the museum.

The museum's operations have also included a whole range of Holocaust-related activities including regular workshops for museum survivor guides, lectures and seminars for Jewish and non-Jewish teachers and students on various aspects of the Holocaust and post-Holocaust issues; the recording of survivor testimony,[63] the organization of travelling exhibitions,[64] books written by Holocaust survivors who migrated to Australia have been launched at the museum; library and archives have to be continually maintained, and the museum has also served as a venue for Second Generation and Child Survivor group meetings. The Centre serves as a host for various other commemorative services, including those that remember *Landsmanschaften* (former inhabitants of towns and settlements in Eastern Europe), *Kristallnacht*, and other special occasions and anniversaries. Films related to the Holocaust are shown at the Centre.

In 1990, six years after opening, the museum had doubled its original size, expanding the existing building to cater for the growing number of visiting groups. By 2003, by which time the museum had again doubled its size following the opening of the new Hadasa and Szymon Rosenbaum Research Centre in 1999, over 260,000 students had visited the Centre.[65] Despite the museum's obvious success, survivors have not become complacent. The persistence of Holocaust denial has been a central incentive for survivor-guides to continue and even intensify their work. 'The Centre is an answer, proof positive, to revisionists who delight in claiming the Holocaust never occurred or is exaggerated.'[66]

Neo-Nazism and Holocaust denial were major triggers leading to the establishment of the Holocaust Institute of WA. The racist activities of the radical right Australian Nationalist Movement were aimed primarily at Perth's Asian community but also included distribution of anti-Semitic posters which stated that the Holocaust was a lie, that it never happened and that 'Jews are running your life'.[67] Many Perth Jews, particularly Holocaust survivors, were deeply disturbed by these events. Ben Korman, a child of Holocaust survivors, was particularly critical of Holocaust denial and revisionism and of the fact that the Holocaust was not taught to WA school students as part of the syllabus. In May 1988 Korman suggested to the Council of Western Australian Jewry (CWAJ) the establishment of a museum to educate the community at large, but especially school students, about the systematic extermination of six million Jews in Europe by the Nazi regime.[68] Although the Holocaust Institute of WA, opened in 1990, was officially established by the CWAJ, its creation was largely due to Korman's unflinching dedication to the project.

The museum only functions due to a handful of Holocaust survivors who relive their painful experiences with each telling of their stories. They are prepared to endure such anguish, firstly, to refute Holocaust denial,[69] secondly, to carry out promises made to those who perished to 'let the world know what happened', and thirdly, in an attempt to educate coming generations so that it will 'never happen again'.[70]

The impact of the Holocaust Institute of WA on Western Australian society is evident from the number of schools attending sessions. Each year approximately 3,000 students tour the museum. Despite limited financial and human resources, the Institute has played a central role in the initiation and organization of a number of educational and commemorative programmes for the Jewish and wider community in Perth, including Holocaust education at Carmel school, travelling exhibitions from interstate,[71] and commemorations and lectures from overseas or interstate Holocaust experts.[72] The Holocaust Institute supported the initiative of Holocaust survivor, Doron Ur, to establish in 1995 a public monument in Supreme Court Gardens, Perth.[73] The monument, in memory of the six million Jews and 600,000 gypsies and others who were murdered by the Nazis, is the site of a short memorial service, held annually on *Yom haShoah.*

As in Melbourne and Perth, Holocaust denial provided a significant impetus behind the processes that eventually led to the creation of the Sydney Jewish Museum too. The success of the 1981 Holocaust Exhibition[74] (which had first been staged in Melbourne), the 1981 International Gathering of Jewish Holocaust Survivors in Jerusalem (attended by over sixty Australian survivors), and the positive responses and interest in the Holocaust which had been generated as a result, provided the stimulus for the establishment of the Association of Jewish Holocaust Survivors (AJHS) in Sydney in 1982.[75] A Holocaust museum was on the agenda of the Association from its outset.

The success of the 1983 American Gathering of Jewish Holocaust Survivors in Washington, a three-day conference that was attended by over 20,000 people, stimulated the AJHS to arrange a similar event in Australia. The concept of an Australian Gathering was spurred on by the perceived extent of Holocaust denial. The president of the AJHS, Albert Halm, was well aware of the dangers inherent in the claims that the Holocaust was a Zionist hoax.[76] Halm stated that 'The fear that pervades our generation is when the survivors are gone and the books of the Holocaust are no longer read, who is likely to believe it really happened?'[77] Many survivors had initially been apprehensive about the planned Australian Gathering but realized that it was time to break their silence and speak about the Holocaust after the League of Rights, a radical right organization, staged a temporary exhibition in Adelaide which included a display which attempted to prove that the Holocaust was a hoax.[78]

Australia's first International Gathering of Jewish Holocaust Survivors was held in Sydney in May 1985 to coincide with the fortieth anniversary of the demise of Nazi Germany and the liberation of the camps. Prominent local and overseas scholars addressed the gathering of about 500 participants on a wide range of Holocaust-related topics.[79] Survivors were disappointed by the perceived apathy of congregations and communal organizations that, according to Halm, repeatedly rebuffed pleas for support.[80] Nonetheless, the AAJHS, which by 1985 had become a national organization, was not deterred from its goal of creating a permanent Holocaust museum in Sydney.[81] In anticipation, the task of collecting and cataloguing artefacts and Holocaust memorabilia was accelerated,[82] and a Museum Committee planned temporary exhibitions about the Holocaust that were staged under the auspices of the NSW Jewish Board of Deputies at the small Jewish Museum in the Great Synagogue.[83] During the 1980s, while the appropriate form and venue for a Holocaust museum were being debated, survivors were involved in a variety of Holocaust remembrance projects which bound them together and simultaneously served to increase informed awareness of the Holocaust in Australian Jewish consciousness. For example, AAJHS activities in 1988 included the production of the *Gift of Life* commemorative book of the 1985 Gathering, a *Kristallnacht* memorial evening was held, survivors continued to volunteer their services to the NSW Board of Deputies' Speaker Service for Sydney's schools, meetings of exhibition guides were convened, books about the Holocaust were launched, a 'Teaching the Holocaust' seminar was held, and Elie Wiesel and Yisrael Gutman addressed the community.[84]

The process of establishing a Jewish Holocaust museum in Sydney was more protracted than in Perth and Melbourne because two benefactors (both Holocaust survivors), Aron Kleinlehrer and John Saunders, who had been unable to work together, had presented the Jewish community with their own, separate museum plans. Eventually, after years of deliberations and negotiations, in November 1992 the Sydney Jewish Museum of Australian Jewish History and the Holocaust was opened. It is first and foremost an educational institution devoted to teaching about the Holocaust and its lessons, in the hope that those events will not be repeated in the future. The permanent exhibition is the focal point around which a wide range of Holocaust related activities, similar to those undertaken in the Melbourne museum, revolve.

The Sydney Jewish Museum has certainly played a major role in increasing awareness of the Holocaust in the general community. By its tenth anniversary, more than 250,000 people had visited the museum, nearly 30,000 in 2001–02 alone.[85] The Sydney Jewish Museum has made a mark on Sydney's cultural landscape as a recognized educational centre and a tourist destination visited by Australian and overseas politicians and diplomats. Paradoxically, only in the last couple of years has Australian Jewry provided the museum with the level of support hoped for by their founders. As has been demonstrated, the Sydney Jewish community was at first sluggish in its support for the survivors' museum project. Although the Holocaust Remembrance committee of the NSW Board of Deputies and the Institute of Holocaust Studies[86] were more closely involved in the latter stages of the founding of the museum, the members of the AAJHS were the main force behind the project from its inception and comprise the majority of its volunteer staff. Only after the death of the museum's benefactor, John Saunders, did the museum become a member of the Jewish Communal Appeal (JCA) which means that it is now largely funded by Sydney Jewry and thus an integral component of the Sydney Jewish community.[87]

There had been a similar apparent lack of broad Jewish community interest in the Melbourne and Perth museums. The *Kadimah* and the Australian Federation of Polish Jews, which initiated the founding of the Jewish Holocaust Museum and Research Centre, were not mainstream Jewish community organizations. Many of the established sections of the Melbourne Jewish community were doubtful of the survivors' plans to establish a Holocaust museum in that city.[88] The *Australian Jewish Times* noted that after two years of operations:

> Apart from individual donations and fundraising by Polish Jews, the communal support for the project has been poor… The Victorian Jewish Board of Deputies held its May meeting at the centre in an effort to focus attention on its importance and its role.[89]

According to Bono Wiener's estimates, as of April 1986 over 90 per cent of Jewish community leadership had still not visited the museum.[90] One devoted volunteer bitterly pointed out that it was not until 1995 that the important work undertaken by the museum was acknowledged at the main communal *Yom haShoah* commemoration.[91] The devoted volunteer staff at the Holocaust Institute also perceived an absence of Jewish community interest. After the Holocaust Institute of WA had been running for seven months, a well-advertised open evening for the Jewish community had to be cancelled because only eight responses were received.

Holocaust survivors not only initiated Holocaust memorialization but led the way in Holocaust education too. Holocaust survivors and their descendants have played a central role in teaching about the Holocaust in Jewish high schools, in providing training and resources for those teaching about the Holocaust in state and private high schools, and in introducing courses about the Holocaust at Australian universities which have attracted large non-Jewish enrolments.[92]

In conclusion, Jewish Holocaust survivors have been the single most significant force in raising Holocaust consciousness in Australia. In particular, they played a central role in the conception, establishment and operations of Holocaust museums in Melbourne, Perth and Sydney. These museums are a testament to the determination and dedication of Holocaust survivors and, in the case of Perth, particularly of one descendant, pursuing their goals despite the initial scepticism of the broader Jewish community. The Australian Jewish leadership played only a supportive role (and sometimes, in the early stages, not even that) in the creation of these museums.

In contrast, the course of Holocaust remembrance in Britain traversed a very different route. Whereas in Australia and New Zealand most major Holocaust remembrance activities were initiated by Holocaust survivors, those in Britain, although supported by Jewish individuals and organizations, emanated mainly from non-Jewish bodies. The interplay between the small number of Holocaust survivors in Britain, the character of Anglo-Jewry and developments in wider British society and culture explain these different paths to Holocaust memorialization.

Anglo-Jewry, more similar in this respect to US than Australian Jewry, deemed that the Holocaust had first to be accepted as significant and relevant by general British society before it could be embraced by Anglo-Jewry.[93] By the last decade of the twentieth century, Second World War experiences were receding from the centre of British consciousness as a new generation, with no direct memories of the war, was coming of age. As the dominant war narratives declined, remembrance of the Holocaust and other tragedies of the Second World War found a place in British culture. From the early 1980s Britain was moving away from a monocultural philosophy towards a more pluralistic vision of British society, one in which more space became available for ethnic and other groups to identify and express themselves openly.[94]

The 1983 Auschwitz Exhibition, supported by the Greater London Council (GLC), Inner London Education Authority (ILEA), British Council of Churches and other charities, and displayed in the Church of St George in the East, is an expression of Britain's gradual adoption of the tenets of multiculturalism. The exhibition, on loan from the Auschwitz Museum in Poland, was brought to the UK by Christians and the Auschwitz Initiative Group, and was locally planned, financed and arranged by the East London Auschwitz Exhibition Committee (ELAEC). It was chaired by the Bishop of Stepney and consisted of members of different faiths and backgrounds. The much visited exhibition, which included parallels between anti-Semitism in Germany in the 1930s and racism in Britain, was accompanied by extensive educational programmes specifically directed to secondary school children in the East London area and organized by a team of local teachers, social workers, former

Auschwitz inmates, and experts in the area. The ELAEC requested support from the Board of Deputies of British Jews: 'I do not need to stress to you the importance of such an exhibit to this area where neo-nazi organizations are emerging to exert considerable influence over the ideas of some of our young white people'.[95] The Board opted to play a 'low key role', preferring the exhibition to appear as the Christian initiative that it was, and not the work of a 'Jewish committee'.[96] It limited its involvement to finding suitable non-Jewish venues throughout the country for the mobile exhibition and providing speakers and educational background material. Indeed, the Board declined taking responsibility for the distribution of the Teaching Pack, *Auschwitz: Yesterday's Racism* (prepared by ILEA), when offered, insisting that such important material should be distributed through the national education authority. This is only part of the story, the other part being that the Board didn't want Holocaust memorialization to be perceived as 'Jewish business'.[97] The exhibition and its accompanying Teaching Pack, although controversial in many respects and eventually withdrawn, was an important first step in anti-racist education which was to be the means by which the Holocaust was to establish its relevance to British society.

The 'Anne Frank' exhibition, which toured the country to great acclaim in 1985–86, was another non-Jewish initiative that also served as a vehicle for anti-racist education and further raised the profile of the Holocaust in general British culture. As Kushner points out:

> They were not isolated events attended largely by Jewish audiences. These exhibitions attracted hundreds of thousands of visitors and were incorporated into school education ... [there was] widespread evidence of general interest in the subject from a younger generation of non-Jewish educationalists ...[98]

Increased interest in the Holocaust from wider British society led the Board of Deputies of British Jews, through its Yad Vashem Committee UK (hereafter YVCUK), to undertake its first serious work on behalf of Holocaust remembrance. Educational resources were made available for schools.[99] Other projects included the linking of British synagogues and communities with *Yad Vashem* in Israel via the Valley of the Lost Communities project, a register of Holocaust survivors in Britain, 'teaching the Holocaust' seminars for teachers, the organization of lectures on the Holocaust, and the publication of survivors' testimonies. Increasing numbers of Holocaust survivors were beginning to speak and publish memoirs of their experiences. This was in part a response to Holocaust

denial literature which surfaced in 1974 with the publication of Richard
Verrall's *Did Six Million Really Die?* and was given particular force by
extreme right-wing, freelance British historian David Irving, who first
denied that Hitler knew anything about the Holocaust and later claimed
that the gas chambers never existed.[100] Rabbi Hugo Gryn broke his silence
and began talking about his experiences of the Holocaust in response to
Holocaust denial. 'It was obscene, people saying that it didn't happen. I
promised myself to talk about it. For too long we were too polite about
what happened.'[101] Auschwitz survivor Kitty Hart had her number cut off
of her arm and preserved it in pickle, which she admits is a 'gruesome
relic' but necessary in face of increasing Holocaust denial.

> As time goes on there are fewer and fewer of us left to testify that
> the abominations did happen; and when we are gone, there must
> be some evidence left so that nobody can hope to get away with
> denying the truth or twisting it to his own ends.[102]

Increased awareness about the Holocaust, together with growing recognition and support for multiculturalism in Britain, combined to provide
the impetus for Greville Janner, QC, MP and Board President, to invest
serious time and energy towards creating a permanent Holocaust
memorial in Britain. After lengthy negotiations with the British government, which included consideration of a number of possible locations,
including the Cenotaph, the Holocaust Memorial Garden was created at
The Dell in Hyde Park in 1983, and became the site for Britain's first
permanent Holocaust memorial in public space. This hesitant assertion
of a particularistic interest reflects the gradual emergence of more
international, post-Holocaust, post-Israel, perceptions of Jewish identity
in Britain.[103]

The most significant turning point in public Holocaust remembrance
in Britain came with the inclusion of education about the Holocaust as
part of the History National Curriculum in 1990. British Jews, most
prominently the Holocaust Education Trust (HET), YVCUK and
Holocaust survivors, had been significant in careful behind-the-scenes
lobbying. They had argued for the Holocaust's relevance to contemporary
British society by tying it to the need for anti-racist education in a
multicultural society. Indeed, the growing climate of ethnic politics in
Britain, more favourable attitudes towards victimhood, and the successes
of previous Holocaust exhibitions (which had also served as vehicles for
anti-racist education) had strengthened their claims. The inclusion of
Holocaust education as part of the National Curriculum had a roll-on

effect in that not only was knowledge of the Holocaust increasingly disseminated to school students but also a demand was created for educational resources, for survivors to speak to school students, and for quality in-service training for teachers of the subject. This need was partly filled by a variety of Jewish community organizations, including the YVCUK, the Weiner Library, the HET and the London Jewish Cultural Centre (LJCC, formerly the Spiro Institute).

It was not only Jewish organizations that responded to the needs of educationalists brought about by the introduction of education about the Holocaust in British schools. The Imperial War Museum (IWM) decided to incorporate a permanent Holocaust gallery. Suzanne Bardgett, project director of the gallery, stated:

> Our decision to mount a permanent exhibition on the Holocaust derives firstly from the conviction that, as we reach the end of the twentieth century, the Holocaust looms as one of the terrible events of our time … Secondly, and on a very practical level, we are responding to a long-standing demand for an exhibition to complement that teaching which now goes on in all secondary schools about the history of Nazi Germany and the Holocaust.[104]

Prior to the announcement of the IWM's project, Anglo-Jewry had been slow to come up with funding and support for a Holocaust museum. According to Ben Helfgott, 'Even a small exhibition couldn't be organized. There was no interest, no one willing to donate time and money.'[105] A 1994 *Jewish Chronicle* editorial refers to 'the inability, or unwillingness, of any of Anglo-Jewry's major organizations or individual philanthropists to take to heart the periodic calls for a museum, or to move beyond intramural differences to join in bringing the proposal to fruition'.[106] However, once the IWM project was announced, and once it was clear that it would be a Holocaust gallery and not an exhibition of 'man's inhumanity to man', Jewish community support was forthcoming. Survivors and various high profile Jewish representatives participated on an Advisory Committee, and Jewish philanthropists promised financial backing. Anglo-Jewry preferred a Holocaust museum to be in public, not 'Jewish space'. One Jewish educationalist commented: '[the IWM] is exactly the right kind of venue for such a museum, if only because of its very non-Jewishness'.[107]

While the concept of a Holocaust gallery at the IWM was being developed, Britain's first Holocaust museum, *Beth Shalom*, a non-Jewish initiative, was opened to great acclaim in Nottinghamshire in 1995. The museum's founder and director, Stephen Smith, son of a Methodist minister, opened the museum 'after being struck by general ignorance about the Holocaust in Britain'.[108] The Smith family conceived, designed, funded and built the museum and education centre in the family's nineteenth-century farmhouse. 1996 saw the opening of the 'Leon Greenman: Auschwitz Survivor 98288' exhibition in the London Museum of Jewish Life in Finchley. In June 2000 the Queen opened the Holocaust gallery in the Imperial War Museum. By the time of the first annual Holocaust Memorial Day on 27 January 2001 the Holocaust was more firmly embedded in British culture.

The original idea for Holocaust Memorial Day in Britain came from Anglo-Jewry but its process of institutionalization needs to be understood in the milieu of interrelated developments in Holocaust education and memorialization in the wider European context.[109] In 1998 Britain had participated in the formation of the Intergovernmental Task Force for Cooperation on Holocaust Education, Remembrance and Research. The following year, a non-Jewish MP, Andrew Dismore, introduced a bill in Parliament 'to introduce a day to learn and remember the Holocaust' after returning from Auschwitz-Birkenau with 150 UK teachers organized by the HET. Following overwhelming support of a Home Office consultation paper,[110] a steering group of government departments and non-governmental organizations (including representatives of a number of Jewish organizations involved in promoting Holocaust remembrance) was set up to implement Britain's decision, announced at the intergovernmental Stockholm Forum in January 2000, to introduce an annual Holocaust Memorial Day.[111] The influence of the Blair government on Holocaust Memorial Day was most significant. One of the electoral promises of New Labour, ulterior motives aside, was a strong moral and ethical platform, including a greater emphasis on immigrant and ethnic rights.[112]

The 2001 Holocaust Memorial Day ceremony at Westminster's Central Hall attracted a capacity 2,000 attendance. Prince Charles and the leaders of Britain's three main political parties joined approximately 200 Holocaust survivors, prominent clergy, many cultural figures, diplomats, and representatives of the Jewish and wider community, hundreds of students and school children. The Holocaust was the main focus but other genocides were remembered too in what was a multicultural, humanitarian occasion. The national event was televised live to approximately one-and-a-half million viewers. Local authorities, community groups, schools and faith groups participated across the country. Events included multi-faith and civic services, seminars, exhibitions, drama, candle-lit vigils, panel discussions, assemblies and more.

Most of the above-mentioned initiatives in the field of Holocaust memorialization and education emanated from non-Jewish institutions or individuals. All received Jewish community support and communal resources and some were a direct result of discreet behind the scenes Anglo-Jewish lobbying. Most Jewish organizations preferred to encourage and support non-Jewish initiatives. They favoured lending a guiding hand. This approach was determined by two interrelated considerations. Firstly, that Holocaust remembrance should not appear as 'Jewish business', and secondly, the perception that the Holocaust had to be accepted as significant by general British culture before it could be fully embraced by Anglo-Jewry.

Indeed, no amount of support, guidance or even pressure could have placed the Holocaust in British culture unless the public was receptive. The British public became increasingly aware of the Holocaust because, throughout the 1990s, Holocaust-related events and activities in Britain and overseas, in addition to those already mentioned, were frequently in the news. The *Kindertransport* reunions, and later the film *Into the Arms of Strangers*, the 1993 opening of the US Holocaust Memorial Museum in Washington DC, the 1994 screening of *Schindler's List*, intense coverage in Britain of the 1995 commemorations of the end of the Second World War and of the liberation of the concentration and death camps, the first national Anne Frank Day in 1996 and the travelling 'Anne Frank in the World' exhibition, the 'Remembering for the Future' international conferences at Oxford (1988 and 2000), the publication of a number of memoirs of British Holocaust survivors and their children, and the mass killings in Rwanda, Bosnia and Kosovo were all catalysts of Holocaust awareness. Indeed, Prime Minister Tony Blair told the Commons that the introduction of Holocaust Memorial Day was given added impetus by evidence of war crimes in Kosovo. There were also various Holocaust-related 'issues' and controversies, including debates over war crime trials, the controversy over Nazi gold in the Swiss banks, the Wilkomirski scandal, slave labour compensation and the libel case between David Irving and Deborah Lipstadt – all heightened interest in the Holocaust and contributed to the momentum which had placed the Holocaust so firmly in British culture.[113] As a result of such an abundance of Holocaust-focused activity, people in Britain began increasingly to perceive the Holocaust as a crisis for European civilization and a continuing issue for all humanity.

The increased centrality of the Holocaust in general British consciousness did not result solely from Jewish attempts to raise the profile of the Holocaust in Britain. As Yehuda Bauer has pointed out, an artificial historical consciousness could not have been created 'without a very real readiness ... to respond to a reminder of the tragedy'.[114] Jewish leaders were only one player among many in memorializing and educating about the Holocaust in Britain. The interest of wider British society in the events of the Holocaust came from the intrinsic power of the events themselves and their relevance to contemporary British social, political and cultural contexts. Jewish individuals and organizations had only to provide the guiding hand. The climate in ethnically diverse Britain was receptive to Holocaust memorialization, especially when it could be utilized for anti-racist education.

What explains these different paths to Holocaust memorialization in Australia, Britain and New Zealand? The processes by which public forms of Holocaust remembrance were established in each country were determined by two main factors – the unique composition of each Jewish community, and the political, social and cultural contexts in the country in which the remembering was taking place. Australian Jewry's significant Holocaust survivor population, spurred on by Holocaust denial to speak publicly about their agonising Holocaust experiences, was the central force behind Holocaust memorialization and education in Melbourne, Perth and Sydney. In contrast, Holocaust survivors comprised a small proportion of Anglo-Jewry where Holocaust memorialization and education were often guided by Jewish individuals and organizations but frequently initiated and implemented by gentiles. While moves to pluralism facilitated Holocaust memorialization in both Australia and Britain, a handful of dedicated survivors have struggled to memorialize and educate about the Holocaust in predominantly bicultural New Zealand. Thus it can be concluded that, quite the opposite from Novick's depiction of developments in the US, Jewish leadership elites played at most a supportive, but certainly not a principal role in Holocaust memorialization in Australia, Britain and New Zealand.

It is far easier to identify the initiators and movers and shakers of Holocaust memorialization than their motivations. Yet, I have found little evidence that Holocaust consciousness was 'artificially fostered' or 'manufactured' for other Jewish objectives as Novick has claimed was the case in the US. I have found only one suggestion that Holocaust memory was being used and abused to raise money for other Jewish causes.[115] I have found little evidence of 'Holocaust programming' aimed primarily at attracting indifferent, assimilating Jews who would not be attracted to the Jewish fold by other approaches. Increased Jewish identity, serving as a barrier to assimilation and intermarriage, has been widely considered a positive by-product but it was not a central motivating force. Although it is likely that some individuals became involved in

Holocaust memorialization to bolster their own self-importance, and some organizations used it to boost their social power, on the whole Holocaust remembrance activities were planned from a genuine feeling of need, duty and obligation to memorialize the six million Jewish victims of Nazism and increase knowledge of the Holocaust in Jewish and general society. Cyla Sokolowicz, editor of the JHM&RC journal, disclosed the primary motivation of Holocaust survivors to volunteer their time to 'programming' Holocaust education and memorialization:

> They are doing it because they believe that their action will influence the way of thinking and feeling of those future adults, that the lessons learned from holocaust survivors will immunize the younger generation against ethnic hatred and persecutions. They are doing it with dedication, precisely because they are volunteers and because no amounts of money paid could make them do it. They are also doing it, because their age reminds them that human life is finite and that they are the last living link with a past that must not be allowed to be forgotten.[116]

As we have seen in this chapter, the importance of transmitting knowledge and memory of the Holocaust became all the more urgent in face of Holocaust denial and the shrinking numbers of survivors. While this chapter focused on the processes whereby the Holocaust entered Jewish and mainstream cultures in Australia, Britain and New Zealand, the following chapter examines whether the representations of the Holocaust in those countries have conveyed its unique or universal aspects.

3

The Uniqueness and Universality
of the Holocaust

The former director of the United States Holocaust Memorial Museum's permanent exhibition, Michael Berenbaum, has argued that, as part of the process of making the museum relevant to non-Jewish Americans the Holocaust had to be 'Americanized', that is, the story of the Holocaust 'had to be told in such a way that it would resonate not only with the survivor in New York and his children in San Francisco, but with a black leader from Atlanta, a Midwestern farmer, or a Northeastern industrialist'.[1] The Americanization, or 'universalization' of the Holocaust, as it is frequently referred to in the literature, involved removing it from an exclusively Jewish context and translating the experience for a wider audience. This chapter is concerned with whether Holocaust memory been similarly universalized in Australia, Britain and New Zealand.[2]

Had the Holocaust been universalized we would expect to find that representations in those countries would include one or more of the following features. Firstly, universalization would involve memories and meanings of the Holocaust being tied to historical experiences of the particular country in which the remembering is taking place. This would include remembrance of national war experiences during the Second World War. The unity and stoicism of Londoners during the Blitz, the heroism of the Battle of Britain, of Dunkirk and of El Alamein could be recalled, as could the victims of Japanese brutality. Skeletal POWs returning home after having survived Changi, forced labour on the Burma Railway, or the forced marches in Sandakan were, for many Anzacs of that generation at least, analogous to the images of concentration camp survivors. Nazi anti-Jewish policies and practice could be contextualized within an extensive Nazi racial programme of mass murder and brutality, thus making the Holocaust relevant to those in Australian, British and New Zealand society identifying with other ethnic or cultural groups persecuted by the Nazis. The focus of remembrance may be on national policy with regard to Jewish refugees prior to, during and following the Holocaust; or it could be on attempts to rescue European Jewry; on the Allied soldiers who participated in the liberation of the camps; or on the refugees from, or survivors of, Nazism who settled in Australia, Britain and New Zealand.

The second aspect of the universalization of the Holocaust involves relating the moral, political and social implications of the Holocaust to current political and social contexts in the country in which the remembering is taking place. As Berenbaum has pointed out, this aspect of the universalization of the Holocaust involves memories of the past interacting with the present to shed light on the future.[3] So, for example, the sufferings of marginal and disadvantaged groups, such as the Aboriginal people in Australia, ethnic minorities in Britain, or the Maoris in New Zealand would be examined. Alternatively, the Holocaust could be remembered within a comparative framework with other genocides, either before or since the Holocaust.

The third aspect of the universalization of the Holocaust involves finding connections and meanings from the Holocaust that are relevant to all people and human experience. This entails consideration of the universal humanistic lessons of the Holocaust, including condemning some behaviours that were common during the Holocaust, such as stereotyping, scapegoating and blind obedience to a state that fosters unethical and immoral acts, while condoning others, including the defence of minority rights, sensitivity to the suffering of others, the critical function of individual responsibility in a democratic society and the imperative to fight against prejudice, discrimination and racism.

The universalization of the Holocaust, which inevitably turns attention away from the destruction of European Jewry, is problematic to many involved in the area of Holocaust remembrance, who fear that it dilutes, blurs and relativises the uniqueness of the Jewish experience under Nazism. Indeed, 'Holocaust' means different things to different people; there is no current consensus on a definition of the term. For most Jews it means the specific Jewish tragedy under Nazism, for others it denotes Nazi mass murder in general, while over the past decade or so, as we shall see in the following chapter, it has come to serve as a metaphor for all of society's ills. Alvin Rosenfeld has warned against this trend 'to metamorphose the Nazi Holocaust into that empty and all but meaningless abstraction, "man's inhumanity to man"'.[4] Rosenfeld 'wonders how any story of the crimes of the Nazi era can remain faithful to the specific feature of those events and at the same time address contemporary American social and political agendas'.[5] Likewise Henryk Grynberg has argued that 'The Holocaust, which was not shared then, cannot be shared now'.[6] Those, like Rosenfeld and Grynberg, who insist on the uniqueness and incomparability of the Holocaust, demand an empiricist approach to its representation, which entails that the story of the Nazi destruction of European Jewry from 1933–45 should be presented as historicist narrative.[7] However, as Rabbi Irving Greenberg understood, this approach is also fraught with risk and can be counter-productive: 'There is a danger of so stressing the uniqueness of the Holocaust that it is turned into a solipsistic event with no consequences or meanings for others.'[8] In other words, Holocaust particularism, stressing the uniqueness of the Holocaust, causes forgetting which is not in line with the aims of its proponents.

Thus it seems that the more the Jewish aspects and lessons are stressed, the greater chance there is that the destruction of European Jewry will be seen as irrelevant, but the more that the Holocaust is shared with wider society, the greater the likelihood that the uniqueness of the Jewish fate will be lost. This paradox in turn brings us to consider the complex issue of motivation. The adoption of a universal approach can be pedagogically sound, the product of a humanistic commitment to educate a broad public about the Holocaust in order to contribute to the building of a more ethical community, but are the motives always authentic? At times the universalist approach has been adopted to deflect the charge of parochialism; at others, to encourage interest in the Holocaust, or even to 'prove' the uniqueness of the Holocaust. For, as Berenbaum has suggested, unique does not mean incomparable:

> the uniqueness of the Jewish experience can best be documented by comparing it with the Nazi treatment of other persecuted populations. Only by understanding the fate of other groups, detailing where it paralleled Jewish treatment and, more import-antly, where it differed, can the distinctive nature of Jewish fate be historically demonstrated.[9]

This chapter examines how debates over the uniqueness and universality of the Holocaust have been reflected in representations of the Holocaust and its meanings at *Yom haShoah* commemorations and Holocaust museums and exhibitions in Australia, Britain and New Zealand. Have divergent national experiences and current realities affected how the Holocaust has been memorialized?

Holocaust commemorations have focused almost exclusively on the Jewish heroes, victims and survivors. For over a decade following the Holocaust, the brave, courageous fighters of the Warsaw Ghetto uprising were the focus of memorial functions. The heroism of the Warsaw

Ghetto fighters was portrayed as a link in the historical and spiritual chain of Jewish resistance to oppression, from the *Maccabees*, through the pogroms in Tsarist Russia, to the rebirth of the Jewish state. At the 1964 commemoration in Wellington, Rev. Silberman recalled generations of persecution '[and then]... out of the glowing of ashes of the crematoria, like the phoenix of mythology, arose a new generation of Jews, young and vigorous, in the revived State of Israel'.[10] This particular emphasis provided a usable past and a source of healthy pride in self-defence, which was something world Jewry needed after the annihilation of two thirds of their people.[11] For at least a decade after the Holocaust, far less attention was devoted to recalling the tragedies and sufferings of the victims in the ghettos and in the concentration camps of Nazi-controlled Europe. Sometimes their passivity was referred to in a negative light. They were condemned for having gone compliantly to their deaths 'like sheep to the slaughter'.[12] Ben Green, Chair of the 1947 Melbourne commemoration, stated that the 'courage of the Jews of the revolt had shown that their people could no longer be slaughtered like sheep but that they would fight for their rights'.[13]

The 1961 Eichmann Trial, which communicated the depths of Nazi bestiality and Jewish suffering in the Holocaust through detailed survivor testimony, together with academic research, which revealed the Nazi state's monopoly on violence, mechanisms of control and tactics of deception, stimulated a more inclusive approach to the memorialization of the Holocaust.[14] The outcome was better appreciation of the circumstances that made physical resistance by European Jewry extremely difficult.[15] Consequently, 'Warsaw Ghetto Day' was broadened and incorporated into the Jewish calendar as 'Martyrs Memorial Day', which continued to commemorate the heroic stand by Warsaw Jewry in 1943, but also served as a permanent memorial to the six million Jews exterminated under Nazism.

The perceived threat of a second Holocaust that accompanied first the 1967 Six Day War and then the 1973 Yom Kippur War led to increased identification with, and understanding of, circumstances of the victims of the Holocaust. Resistance to Nazism was re-defined and expanded to include the fight for spiritual and physical survival. The victims' attempts to survive and maintain human and Jewish dignity in intolerable circumstances became known as 'spiritual resistance' or the 'heroism of daily life'. Over the last decade *Yom haShoah* commemorations have focused not only on the varied responses and experiences of the six million Jewish victims of the Holocaust but also on the survivors. Increased knowledge about the Holocaust, and Jewish responses to it, together with the realization that the survivors are ageing, led to a growing regard from Jewish communities for those who are still able to tell their stories. Survivors, aware of the power of eye-witness testimony in countering Holocaust denial, became more willing to speak publicly about their experiences. The incorporation of testimony of survivors in *Yom haShoah* commemorations in Australia, Britain and New Zealand, is one of the few ways in which the events of the Holocaust were linked to the country in which the remembering was taking place.

As we have seen, over time *Yom haShoah* commemorations broadened to convey a plurality of Jewish experiences[16] of the Holocaust, but the wider context of the Second World War was usually recalled only in order to demonstrate the silence of the Western world to the evolving Final Solution. The alleged lack of serious attempts at rescue or retaliation by the 'civilised' world during the Holocaust was frequently condemned, particularly the failure of the Allies to bomb Auschwitz and other Nazi camps, and the lack of aid provided to the Warsaw Ghetto fighters.[17] Church leaders, specifically Pope Pius XII and the Vatican, were criticized for their failure to denounce the Nazi regime or more actively protect the Jews. The Allied and neutral governments were rebuked for closing their doors to Jewish refugees, as was the Red Cross for its failure to censure Nazi atrocities.

At London's 1963 commemoration, Dayan M. Steinberg, former Senior Jewish Chaplain to the Polish Forces in the British Eighth Army, asserted that the accusations sometimes made against Jews for their alleged passivity in face of death should have been directed against the world that was silent while such events happened in the heart of Europe.[18] At Melbourne's 1966 commemoration, Abba Kovner, an Israeli poet and partisan, asserted that 'We have nothing to be ashamed of in the memory of our martyrs... The eternal shame lies on those who could have helped but didn't'.[19] In Auckland, Dr Geoffrey Levy depicted the passivity of the Western world to Nazi anti-Semitism, and concluded: 'On all sides we stood alone'.[20]

The Holocaust has only rarely been connected to the experiences of British and ANZAC soldiers or even to the memories and experiences of the one and a half million Jewish men and women of the Allied Forces who helped defeat the Nazis. Occasionally one of the 'Righteous Among the Nations',[21] or the liberators are remembered and honoured, but in the main non-Jewish victims of Nazism have been excluded from memorial evenings.[22] As Pierre Nora has reminded us with depressing pessimism, 'Memory is blind to all but the group it binds'.[23] The sufferings of other victim groups under Nazism were perceived as tragic but different from the uniqueness of the Jewish Holocaust. An outcome of this narrow focus is a correspondingly narrow consideration of the lessons of the Holocaust that have tended to focus on the Jewish lessons to the exclusion of consideration of the universal humanistic ones.

The perception of the abandonment of the Jews under Nazism led many Jews worldwide to conclude that Jews must defend themselves as they must 'never again' depend on others for protection. The 'Zionist lesson of the Holocaust', that a sovereign Jewish state would prevent a recurrence of the events that led to the Holocaust, reverberated through Holocaust commemorations and was the most consistent response to the outcry 'Never Again'. This understanding was clearly articulated by Joe Berinson at Perth's 1972 commemoration.

> The second and perhaps most important lesson of the period is the centrality of a Jewish State to the possibility of Jewish survival. There was nowhere for the Jews of the European ghettos to go. If God forbid, another Hitler does appear his victims will at least have somewhere to turn.[24]

Yet the relationship between Israel and the Diaspora would be reciprocal – all Jews, whether they be religious or secular, orthodox or liberal, male or female, had an obligation to work together for the security of the State of Israel.[25]

Successive threats to Israel's security further intensified the perception that the world was, and remains, relatively indifferent to the fate of Jews and that, as a consequence, the Jewish people could rely only on their own resources. The 1967 Six Day War, the 1973 Yom Kippur War and terrorist attacks against Jews in Israel and overseas produced tensions that were released at Holocaust commemorations. The Zionist lesson of the Holocaust was expressed with even more certainty than usual. At Perth's 1973 *Yom haShoah* commemoration, Dr Albert Gild asserted that six years after the 1967 war, Jews stand united and determined that there shall never again be a Warsaw Ghetto.[26] Both past and present Jewish isolation and vulnerability were very much at the forefront of Isi Leibler's consciousness when he asserted, 'when the chips are down we must rely on ourselves and not on the consciences of governments ... The only escape from the final solution is that we act alone to save ourselves'.[27] The words of an Israeli soldier, repeated at a commemoration in London, demonstrates how remembrance of the Holocaust and concern for the continued existence of the State of Israel were inextricably linked.

> When I found myself on the canal alone, and coming towards me
> was a host of tanks and men, I saw only one thing – the number
> tattooed on your arm, the number from Auschwitz, and that helped
> me to stand my ground and not to give up.[28]

The traumatic Jewish past was continuing to exert a powerful influence
on the present.

The Zionist lesson of the Holocaust predominated but was not the
only lesson conveyed at *Yom haShoah* commemorations. A second lesson
derived from remembrance of the Holocaust was that each Jew in the
Diaspora must be vigilant to anti-Semitism and neo-Nazism in order to
prevent a recurrence of the events that led to the Holocaust. For two
decades following the end of the Second World War the main threat of
anti-Semitism was perceived as coming from an economically, politically
or militarily rejuvenated West Germany. Efforts of the US and the West
to integrate West Germany as an ally in the Cold War alarmed many
Jews. The rehabilitation and rearmament of West Germany against the
allegedly aggressive Soviet Union stirred widespread Jewish fear of
German 'renazification'. Many commemoration addresses during the
1950s conveyed the message that the rehabilitation of West Germany as
a world power should be opposed and attempts to 'forgive and forget'
what they considered to be the responsibility of the German people for
Nazism should be condemned. References to 'the forces of evil which
are preparing to rise again', were frequent.[29] At the 1954 commemoration
in London, organized by the British–Polish Friendship Society, Alec
Wasserman declared:

> Unless we draw proper conclusions from what happened in the
> Ghetto in Warsaw and in other ghettoes [sic] the commemoration
> of the heroic uprising becomes a fraud. History may repeat itself in
> one or another form. We cannot commemorate the ghetto and yet
> do nothing about German rearmament and the H-bomb.[30]

The maintenance of business contacts and personal relations with
Germans, especially individuals who bought German goods, was also
denounced. 'If we Jews do it, if we trade with Germany, we shall be traitors
to our own blood', said Rabbi Sanger in Melbourne.[31] Australian Jewry also
condemned the Australian Federal Government's plans to bring 'the
murderers of the Warsaw Ghetto victims as migrants to Australia'.[32]

By the late 1950s and early 1960s, the subject of German 'renazification' was gradually fading as links between Israel and West Germany

increased, the democratization of West Germany became evident, and reparations were paid to some Jewish Holocaust survivors.[33] However, new threats to Jewish survival emerged in the 1960s and 1970s. These came not only from 'the Arab world' but also from its 'leftist' sympathizers, and the USSR and her satellites. Anti-Semitism was re-emerging as anti-Zionism.

In response, speakers at *Yom haShoah* commemorations, guided by the resistance of the ghetto fighters and perhaps also by the perception that Jews in the democratic West had not done enough to help European Jewry during the Holocaust,[34] stressed even more than at previous commemorations the case for Jewish unity and the imperative to provide aid to Jews overseas who faced spiritual and physical persecution.[35] It was pointed out that as the Mizrachi, Zionists, Socialists and others had all stood together to revolt against Nazism, so too should world Jewry stand united against anti-Semitism and neo-Nazism. Holocaust commemorations were considered appropriate forums to promote the campaign to 'free' the *refusenik* Jews of the Soviet Union, those whose applications to leave the country had been denied and who consequently faced persecution, and according to one New Zealander, 'cultural genocide'.[36] In Sydney in 1971 NSW Hillel Director, Rabbi Mattis Kantor, asserted that the Warsaw Ghetto 'is one of the historical precedents for Soviet Jews that their present defiance will result in an ultimate freedom'.[37]

Whereas in Australia and New Zealand, the call for Jewish mutual aid was applied to the alleviation of the plight of Soviet Jewry, in Britain there was concern about anti-Semitism facing the tiny remnant of Jews in Poland.[38] Almost all speeches at the 1968 commemoration in London decried the anti-Semitic campaign by the Polish authorities as a revival of the spirit of which the Holocaust was the outcome. Simon Frisner, chairman of PJEX (Polish-Jewish Ex-Servicemen's Association), condemned the Polish attempt to make the tiny surviving remnant of Polish Jewry the scapegoats for the regime's internal difficulties. 'The accusations against Jews of disloyalty to their native land are tragically reminiscent of the savage attacks made against Jewry by both Hitler and Stalin in the past.'[39] Indeed, Anglo-Jewry broke with tradition and did not invite the Polish ambassador to the 1968 commemoration in protest over Polish anti-Semitism.[40] Through the 1970s and 1980s *Yom haShoah* commemorations were a platform for the expression of outrage at a range of incidents indicating the continued existence of Polish anti-Semitism. The absence of a Jewish pavilion at Auschwitz,[41] Polish perpetuation of the myth that the Warsaw Ghetto fighters received 'massive' outside help,[42] and the building of convents and chapels in

Auschwitz provided focus points for *Yom haShoah* speeches.[43] The overriding message was that world Jewry should unite and not remain silent in face of continued Polish anti-Semitism.

We have seen that Holocaust commemorations conveyed the messages that the recurrence of the Holocaust could best be avoided by Jewish self-reliance – by vigilance to anti-Semitism and neo-Nazism, by Jewish unity to aid Jews suffering spiritual and physical persecution, and most importantly, by self-defence in the form of a sovereign Jewish state. Yet 'Never Again', which reverberated at all Holocaust commemorations, has the potential to instruct much more. It can be applied to the prevention or alleviation of human suffering of any people anywhere. It can be used to convey universal humanistic lessons of the Holocaust – 'Never Again' should racism, bystanderism, xenophobia, discrimination, stereotyping, intolerance and other of evils associated with Nazism confront humankind. Has the perceived silence of much of the Western world and Church during the Holocaust led those addressing the commemorations to convey that bystanderism is morally repugnant and must not be repeated in face of current and future genocidal situations? Has the memory of those Nazi anti-Jewish policies, which evolved into the Final Solution, been interpreted as bearing any message to Jews to join the struggle against later expressions of discrimination, persecution and racism in the world?

An analysis of the transmission of universal humanistic lessons of the Holocaust revealed only differences of degree between Jewish communities in Australia, Britain and New Zealand. Although Australian Jews often repeat the phrase that 'the Holocaust was unique but its lessons were universal', this universalism has rarely been explored at Australian *Yom haShoah* commemorations. References to contemporary genocides, human rights abuses, affronts to justice and freedom, and racist activity in Australia or elsewhere were not a significant component of Holocaust commemoration speeches in Melbourne, Perth or Sydney from 1945 until the mid-1990s. The oft-repeated phrase, 'Never Again', seems to have had a restricted applicability to the Jewish people, and not to the prevention or alleviation of human suffering of any people, anywhere.

The response to Liberal Senator Peter Baume's appeal to Jews to speak out and act in defence of people threatened with genocide at Melbourne's 1986 *Yom haShoah* commemoration illustrates Australian Jewry's narrow understanding of the lessons of the Holocaust.[44] Baume, who had made specific reference to genocidal acts in Kampuchea, Uganda, Zimbabwe and Ethiopia, was criticized by the Chairman of the Victorian Jewish Board of Deputies, Sam Wolski, who 'found a problem with what Senator Baume said because he described the Holocaust as not a Jewish problem',[45] and had not conveyed what Wolski referred to as the 'true message' of the Holocaust.[46]

Those attending commemorations in London were quite frequently urged by Jewish and non-Jewish speakers to continue the legacy of the ghetto fighters by combating discrimination and racial or other persecution, wherever it might occur. For example, in the context of race violence which was plaguing Britain throughout the 1960s, B. Gillis, vice-president of World Jewish Congress (British Section) (WJC, BS) and Anglo-Jewish Ex-Servicemen's Association (AJEX), insisted that the message of the ghetto fighters must be continued by uniting in opposition to all forms of hatred and prejudice anywhere:

> we may gain from these tragic happenings a lesson to guide us in the years ahead – a lesson which will safeguard the new world, ensure that these things will never happen again. At all times we must recognize our responsibilities to our neighbours, locally, nationally and internationally. We must recognize that mankind is not divided by race, by colour or by religion, but that all men [sic] form together one great human body and when untied can undoubtedly march forward to the Golden Age.[47]

This type of vague and unspecific statement was fairly typical. Reginald Freeson and his predecessor as Chair of the Memorial Committee, Michael Cliffe MP, were rare exceptions in conveying the message that it was imperative to stand up and fight when not only Jews, but also any other minority was under attack because of its race, colour or religion. For example, in 1966 Freeson insisted that the neo-Nazis who had been convicted of burning synagogues in Britain must be dealt with the utmost severity of the law, but added that 'We must concern ourselves with the synagogue fires ... but we must also show our concern when coloured people are being shot at from speeding cars in the streets of London'.[48]

Following a march by the National Front through the streets of Lewisham, the vice-president of AJEX, Cecil Hyams, confidently declared: 'the Union Jack, under which we fought and died, will never become the property of the street bully boy'.[49] In line with the sentiments of the organization being represented, this expression of patriotism considered the lessons of the Holocaust from a British, more than a Jewish, perspective. Yet these responses from Freeson, Hyams and a handful of others over the years should not be taken out of perspective.

Speakers rarely urged those attending to apply universal humanistic lessons of the Holocaust to contemporary contexts in Britain or elsewhere. *Yom haShoah* commemorations in London, in common with those in Australia, have still focused predominantly on the Jewish lessons of the Holocaust.

The fortieth anniversary commemorations of the liberation of the death camps, which were open to the public and attended by thousands, was a major public event in Wellington in 1985. The occasion was organized by a sub-committee of the New Zealand Jewish Council and was supported by a range of other Jewish and non-Jewish groups.[50] The aim of the organizing committee was outward looking.

> To ensure the participation and interest of the community at large, the function has been deliberately structured to reflect not merely the Jewish experience but also the experience of the millions of Christians and others who suffered as a result of the Nazi's [*sic*] programme of extermination on racial or religious grounds.[51]

In line with these aims, the commemorative event included remembrance of other victims of Nazism (including gypsies, intellectuals and homosexuals), addresses by non-Jewish public figures, and a presentation to a Righteous Gentile. The keynote speaker, Edith Eger, a Holocaust survivor and international consultant on human behaviour, included in her speech a condemnation of the tyranny of totalitarian regimes. Whereas the annual commemorations traditionally ended with the *Hatikvah*, the Israeli national anthem, this one ended with God Save New Zealand.

The success of the 1985 commemoration in Wellington gave the Auckland Jewish community confidence to host a public commemoration of the fiftieth anniversary of the Warsaw Ghetto Uprising in 1993. This important event was suitably marked by the unveiling of Auckland's Holocaust Memorial, a sculpture that depicted the crimes of the Nazis as well as the neglect and apathy of much of the world to the events of the Holocaust.[52] The Governor General, Government of New Zealand, Embassy of Israel, City of Auckland and justice system were all represented at this key event and many church leaders, politicians, police, defence chiefs and media also attended. The subject matter of speeches was not confined to Jewish aspects of the Holocaust and its meanings. Ruth Filler, Chair of the Holocaust Memorial Project Committee, spoke about the need to preserve the freedom and dignity of individuals, child survivor Robert Narev expressed gratitude for the respect for religious and cultural identity in New Zealand, while Arnold Zable, a guest speaker from Australia, warned against racism and ethnic cleansing in the world, and Lesley Max commented on the growth of racism in New Zealand. These universal lessons would surely have resonated with the general public that attended the open commemoration.

Yet, as with Freeson and Hyams' speeches in London, these two public events were the exceptions to Holocaust memorialization in New Zealand. Commemorations in Auckland and Wellington, which were typically closed Jewish community affairs, seldom universalized the Holocaust.[53] As with commemorations in Australia and Britain, the focus of remembrance was almost exclusively on the six million Jewish victims of Nazism and most interpretations of the meaning of the Holocaust fell into the Jewish categories outlined earlier.

The reason for this restricted focus lies in two factors. Firstly, the widespread sense that European Jewry had been abandoned by Western civilization caused resentment and led many to reject Judaism's universal mission and to concentrate on Jewish issues and agendas.[54] Secondly, the nature of the memorial evening determined its narrow focus. The intense grief of survivors and those who lost their friends and relatives in the Holocaust created a solemn atmosphere of mourning during which many of those attending were aware that it really could have happened to them, for the Final Solution meant not only the destruction of European Jewry but prospectively the extermination of the Jewish people worldwide.[55] Many Australian, British and New Zealand Jews are conscious that they escaped the fate of European Jewry due to their ancestors' timely migration. Speaking at the 1970 Melbourne commemoration, Henry Shaw, Hillel Director, related to the audience how he asked himself: 'Why have I survived when 65 of my cousins died in Poland; why have I, conceived in Lodz and born by accident in London, survived?'[56] These understandings have united Jewish communities in remembrance of the Jewish heroes and victims of the Holocaust and in consideration of the Jewish lessons of the Holocaust. They have mourned and identified what could have been their own past in the group's shared memories of that event.

Indeed, this intense atmosphere of grief is one of the reasons determining that commemorations in Australia have been consciously preserved as Jewish community affairs. Another reason is the fear that open commemorations will lead to loss of control. This was most apparent in Birmingham in 1977 when the city's Lord Mayor, Councillor Harold Powell, insensitively told a Holocaust remembrance commemoration that it was time for the Jews to forget and forgive the Germans.[57] There have been few negative repercussions following the introduction of an annual Holocaust Memorial Day in Britain. Yet, the danger exists that the organizers of future

Holocaust Memorial Day commemorations may choose to focus on sufferings, such as the alleged 'Palestinian holocaust', that are potentially harmful to Anglo-Jewry. Fearful of scenarios such as these, Australian Jewry has refrained from opening commemorations to the wider public.

In conclusion, the predominantly closed, inward-looking commemorations have determined a Judeocentric approach to the Holocaust and its lessons. Would we then expect to find a broader representation of the Holocaust at exhibitions and museums that were specifically directed at general society? Has the Holocaust has been universalized in Holocaust museums and exhibitions in Australia, Britain and New Zealand?

Jewish Holocaust museums in Australia are somewhat more outward looking than the parochial *Yom haShoah* commemorations but still, until recently, the Holocaust had rarely been universalized. All three Holocaust museums in Australia defined the event as the systematic annihilation of European Jewry, unequivocally asserting the uniqueness of Jewish suffering and fate. Established to inform the Jewish and wider Australian public about the Holocaust, doing so at a time when the existence of the gas chambers was being denied, the museums focus on the events that overcame European Jewry from 1933 to 1945.[58]

The uniqueness of the Holocaust predominates at all these museums and sets the tone for how the sufferings of others under Nazism are addressed. At the JHM&RC a section entitled 'Non-Jewish Victims' asserts that between thirty-five and fifty million people were killed during the Second World War. Yet the text also insists 'The tragedy that befell the Jewish people was unique in its intent and dimensions'.[59] The Sydney Jewish Museum includes information about the non-Jewish victims of Nazism in three sections but the uniqueness of Nazi anti-Jewish policy is unambiguous: 'What makes the Holocaust unique is not just the gigantic scale of the killing. The annihilation of the Jews was an enterprise of the state, a genocide by government policy, carried out in a systematic and machine-like manner.'[60] Similarly, guides at the Holocaust Institute of WA emphasize the uniqueness of Nazi anti-Jewish policy:

> the Final Solution included the *whole* of European Jewry, a total of 11 million Jews were identified for extermination. No other ethnic or cultural group was identified for systematic annihilation by the Nazis in this way.[61]

The differences between extermination camps (equipped with special installations) and concentration camps is also stressed at the Holocaust Institute of WA. The students learn that:

> The distinction is very important. Comparisons can be drawn with concentration camps. There is NOTHING comparable with the Extermination or Death Camps – not before the Holocaust and not since![62] [capitals in original]

Guides point to a map to distinguish between the six death camps in Poland where Jews were systematically annihilated, from the concentration camps, where inmates were used as slave labourers, deprived of their freedom, starved, beaten and sometimes murdered. The guides explain that concentration camp inmates included not only Jews, but also Poles, Sinti and Roma (Gypsies), Soviet Prisoners of War, the handicapped, psychiatric patients, homosexuals, Jehovah's Witnesses, Freemasons and others whom Nazi ideology identified as either racially and biologically 'inferior', or politically undesirable. In this way, the Holocaust Institute, in common with the JHM&RC and the Sydney Jewish Museum, acknowledges the suffering of others under Nazism while delineating a clear hierarchy of victimization.

It could be assumed that the detailed inclusion of the tragedies of other groups persecuted by the Third Reich would interest and attract Australians identifying with those ethnic or cultural groups and consequently make the museums more relevant to the Australian social environment, but the emphasis on the uniqueness of the Holocaust has meant that the other victims of Nazism have not been a significant feature of the museums. The same emphasis also explains the lack of references to Australian experiences of the Second World War. Parallels between the fate of the Jews under Nazism and the sufferings of Australian POWs under the Japanese, in Changi, the Burma Railway or Sandakan, for example, have not been drawn, even though this may have made the museums more relevant to broader Australian society as, in Anglo-Australian eyes of that generation at least, there are parallels between German and Japanese aggression and brutality.

The narratives of Holocaust museums in Australia avoid any explicit references to other genocides either before or since the Holocaust. The experiences of the Jews during the Holocaust have not been related to the sufferings of Aboriginal people in Australia. The torment of Aborigines in Australia is not mentioned in the museums' texts even though information about their suffering could have made the museums more directly relevant to the Australian public. Indeed, a 1995 proposal to change the name of the 'Sydney Jewish Museum of Australian Jewish History and the Holocaust' to the 'Australian Holocaust Museum'[63] was rejected by museum staff, who feared the name change would lead to pressure on the museum to incorporate the tragedies of other peoples, and the histories of other genocides – a move, it was claimed, which would threaten the uniqueness of the Holocaust and eventually lead to the loss of the museum's Jewish focus.[64]

This Australian approach, which concentrates on narrating the events which overcame European Jewry from 1933 to 1945, has been encapsulated by Sylvia Rosenblum, curator of the Sydney Jewish Museum: 'The Holocaust must not be manipulated ... One cannot use the Holocaust to tell other stories ... The task of Holocaust museums is to tell the story of the Holocaust simply, truthfully and honestly so that it would never happen again.'[65] This distinctive Australian approach derived from several interrelated factors.

Since Jewish Holocaust museums in Australia were financed by private Jewish funds and established predominantly by Holocaust survivors, no outside political pressures affected the museums' representations. The overwhelmingly Jewish design teams, expressing the non-universalistic outlook of Australian Jewry, agreed that the story of the Holocaust should be told from the perspective of the Jewish victims. Their museums would not include detailed representations of other Nazi victims, of Australian victims of Japanese brutality during the Second World War, or information about victims of other human tragedies before or after the Holocaust. Australian Jewry, increasingly self confident and relatively free from anti-Semitism in multicultural Australian society, did not perceive a need to universalize or 'Australianize' the Holocaust to make it relevant to the non-Jewish public.

The universal lessons of the Holocaust have been partially explored in Holocaust museums in Australia. Museum guides, and even some of the exhibition texts, have condemned racism, prejudice, bystanderism and indifference to suffering, and intolerance. Students have been urged to utilize their democratic rights to prevent the emergence of totalitarian regimes and to protect human rights. Yet humanistic and universal values were conveyed only as they emanated directly from the specific story of the Jewish catastrophe. Guides have rarely urged visitors to apply their lessons on racism and genocide to analogous contemporary issues in Australia or elsewhere.

However, from about the mid-1990s, the aims of Holocaust museums in Melbourne and Sydney evolved to include not only education about the events that overcame European Jewry between 1933 and 1945, but also transmission of universal humanistic lessons of the Holocaust. Jonathan Morris, the JHM&RC's Executive Officer since 2002, asserts that the museum serves not only as a memorial but also for teaching future generations about the horrors of anti-Semitism, racial intolerance and xenophobia.[66] The museum's activities have broadened according to these aims. The museum's staff are not only concerned with racism when it is anti-Semitism, rather, their sensitivity to anti-Semitism has extended to racism directed at others. As is detailed in chapter six, the museum's programme for the Jewish and wider community, which was initially limited to educational sessions on specific aspects on the Holocaust and seminars for Victorian school teachers on 'Teaching the Holocaust', has developed to include educational sessions about combating racism. In recognition of these activities, the Centre received a highly prestigious Victorian Award for Excellence in Multicultural Affairs in 2002. John Landy, Victorian State Governor, presented the award, stating 'This important Museum and Research Centre is Victoria's finest memorial to the victims of racist policies'.[67] Smuel Rozenkranz, the Centre's President, stated 'It is, indeed an honour ... it will spur on our activities in ensuring that we continue to combat these ills and diseases that are today, including in Australia, causing hatred and racism'.[68] Indeed, the anti-racist message appears to be reaching students. Research undertaken at the Centre by Dr Susanne Wright, revealed that when asked 'What best describes how you feel about the personal stories told by the guides', one in four students included 'they showed me what racism really means'.[69] One student commented 'Like the guide said "The only race is the human race". I am very moved by the line because I, myself, am a Chinese and I feel "accepted" once again'.[70] Dr Wright concluded 'This research confirms the valuable contribution the Centre makes not only to the greater understanding of the Holocaust in historic and personal terms, but also issues of human rights and anti-racism in general'.[71]

Holocaust museums may also be changing their approach to the representation of Aboriginal suffering in Australia. In 2002 the JHM&RC organized a function to commemorate a group of Aborigines who in 1938, a few weeks after *Kristallnacht*, protested to the German consul in Melbourne about the treatment of Jews in Nazi Germany. Keynote speaker, Justice Marcus Einfeld, paid respects to the courage and humanity of William Cooper and the Australian Aborigines' League who had protested even though they were not recognized as Australians at that time. Einfeld asserted: 'We continue to deny indigenous people the very equal opportunity to a fair chance in life', and asserted that it was a Jewish obligation to fight racism in Australia.[72]

The Sydney Jewish Museum is equally committed to educating against racism and to conveying other universal, humanistic messages of the Holocaust. The most recent collection of educational materials produced by the museum, *Teaching the Holocaust* by Sophie Gelski, is a compilation of lesson plans, resource and background materials that enable and support teachers wishing to educate about the Holocaust, anti-racism, human rights and civics and citizenship.[73] Lesson plans challenge students to evaluate moral and ethical action across religious and philosophical boundaries and subsequently re-evaluate their personal motivations and decisions.[74] The Holocaust Institute in Perth is currently considering similarly placing greater emphasis on the universal lessons of the Holocaust as its committee contemplates possible directions for the museum in the absence of survivors in the not so distant future. In taking on the task of anti-racist education Holocaust museums in Melbourne and Sydney have translated the lessons of the Holocaust to the national context in which the race debate, brought to the forefront of Australian politics by One Nation, has been re-ignited by issues surrounding refugees and asylum seekers.

As with Holocaust museums in Australia, those in Auckland and Wellington provide a chronological narrative of the events that over-came European Jewry between 1933 and 1945. One of the opening panels at the permanent Holocaust exhibition in the Auckland War Memorial implies the uniqueness of the Holocaust:

> The Holocaust is presented here as a Jewish experience. This is not to deny the reality of the sufferings of millions of other victims of the Third Reich. They are also honoured and remembered … But Hitler's war was also a war against the Jews – for no other reason that that [*sic*] they were Jews.

The events of the Holocaust are made relevant to wider New Zealand society through the stories, artefacts and art works of survivors who settled in New Zealand.[75] Most of the survivors featured are Jewish but one is Maori, Tahu Hopkinson, who served with New Zealand's Maori battalion: 18 Platoon. In this way the exhibition is linked to the 'Remembering New Zealanders at War', *Scars on the Heart*, permanent exhibition.

Interpretation of the meanings of the events is, in the main, left to each individual visitor, but a number of short axioms, which may inspire consideration of the universal lessons of the Holocaust, are positioned above each section. 'Racism is man's greatest threat to man – the maxi-mum of hatred for the minimum of reason', has been placed above the exhibition's depiction of life in the ghettos. The section about the Final Solution includes a famous quote from Heinrich Heine (1823): 'That was only a prelude, where they burn books, in the end it is people they burn'. Elsewhere the visitor is challenged by Edmund Burke's warning: 'The only thing necessary for the triumph of evil is for good men to do nothing.' At the exhibition's opening in 1998, the lessons of the Holocaust were clearly connected to the lives of its overwhelmingly non-Jewish visitors. Andrew Krukziener, child of the Holocaust survivors who were the exhibition's main benefactors, asserted:

> Prejudice is wrong. The acceptance of different religious races or creeds is important; People are people; The stereotyping of different races or religions is a dangerous start to a disastrous end; Be prepared to question authority. Rules are not always right; Use you own morality as the judge and fight injustice wherever you are. I owe it to the memory of my ancestors to ensure that something like the holocaust never happens again, not only to Jews but to anybody... It is my hope that, in some small way, this Holocaust exhibition opened here today, may educate people, that victimization and persecution of any minority, is evil.[76]

The uniqueness and universality of the Holocaust are similarly represented at the Holocaust exhibition in Wellington's Jewish Centre, which was established almost single-handedly in 1989 by Holocaust survivors Hanka and George Pressburg. School, service, church and community groups visit the modest exhibit as part of a Jewish cultural tour that is organized by the Council of Jewish Women.[77] The display about the Holocaust includes memorabilia, photographs, money from a ghetto, identification papers, yellow stars and a concentration camp uniform. However, the centrepiece of the visit is, undoubtedly, the groups' meeting with a Holocaust survivor. Hanka, who tells her story most weeks, instructs students that it is the 'unprecedented murder of innocent children plus the use of technology in the gas chambers which set the Holocaust apart as a uniquely dark episode in human history'.[78] Hanka, who recognizes that other groups were victimized by Nazism, always acknowledges the liberating armies and the various non-Jews who helped her to survive at various stages of her ordeals. Hanka stresses that the Holocaust was unique but that its lessons are universal. Through her experiences of persecution and discrimination Hanka conveys a firm message of the necessity of tolerance of differences in New Zealand society.[79]

Britain has three permanent Holocaust museums – Beth Shalom Holocaust Memorial Centre (1995), the Leon Greenman exhibition in the London Museum of Jewish Life (1996), and the Holocaust exhibition at the Imperial War Museum (IWM) (2000).[80] Although British Jews, including historians and Holocaust survivors, were, to varying degrees, involved in the curation and operations of Beth Shalom and the IWM, they were initiated and established by gentiles. In contrast, the permanent 1996 Leon Greenman exhibition in the London Museum of Jewish Life in Finchley was a Jewish initiative and Jewish people predominated in its establishment process and operations. How have their diverse origins impacted on the museums' representations of the Holocaust? And in what ways are they similar to, or different from, Holocaust museums in Australia and New Zealand?

The universalization of the Holocaust is evidenced through the essential concept, narrative, artefacts and educational programmes of the 'Leon Greenman: Auschwitz Survivor 98288' exhibition. This exhibition on the rise of Nazism and the Holocaust is told through the life story of Leon Greenman, a British citizen and Holocaust survivor, who was born in London's East End. Many of Leon's own photographs and personal possessions are featured, including his wife's wedding dress, his concentration camp uniform and mementos belonging to his son Barney. Besides appearing at the museum, on request, to provide personal testimony to groups, Leon continues to fight racist injustice of all kinds. His message is: 'Young and old alike must learn about the the [*sic*] Holocaust as a warning against the dangers of racism. There is no difference in colour or religion.'[81]

Responses of visitors indicate that lessons are being conveyed implicitly through the text. One student wrote:

> The trip made a lasting impression … It has changed my outlook towards racism, no longer will I sit back and let people make racist comments or jokes in my presence. I feel it is no-one's right to judge another person by their colour or race.[82]

Designed to suit pupils at Key Stage 3 and 4, GCSE and Advanced Level as part of their National Curriculum studies, the exhibition has an accompanying Resource Book that suggests that teachers lead students to grapple with probing questions and dilemmas. Students are asked to consider why so many turned a blind eye to persecution and torture happening right in front of them while only a minority risked their own lives by becoming rescuers. The universal messages of the Holocaust are translated into the students' own world by leading them to consider issues surrounding peer pressure, the need to be part of a crowd, the fear of those who are different. It is suggested that teachers explore specific scenarios relating to the area of scapegoating with their students. The emphasis is on creating empathy as a means for identification and prevention in the future. The resource material guides teachers to consider the universal humanistic lessons of the Holocaust; no mention is made to specifically Jewish ones. Although the 'uniqueness' of the Holocaust is not mentioned, the narration of Leon's personal story is set within the wider context of the evolving Final Solution and the consequent destruction of European Jewry.

The Holocaust exhibition in the IWM also uses Holocaust survivor testimony, together with film, photographs, models, maps, diagrams, books, posters, artefacts, old newsreels and other films, and documents, to enrich its chronological narrative of the Holocaust – defined as the Nazis' attempted annihilation of European Jewry. Punctuating the exhibition at nine different points are excerpts from testimonies of fifteen Holocaust survivors who settled in Britain after the Second World War. For example, the personal experiences of Rabbi Hugo Gryn and Roman Halter enhance the section on deportation, while the Auschwitz section includes testimony from Kitty Hart-Moxton who was incarcerated in the camp with her mother. Britain's connection to the Holocaust is not restricted to the experiences of those who settled in Britain after the war. The ways in which news of the Holocaust reached Britain is covered in a series of four showcases entitled 'News Reaches Britain', 1939–40, 1941–43, 1943–44, 1945, which link the evolving Nazi anti-Jewish policy to events in Britain. 'News Reaches Britain, 1945' consists of British newspaper reports, photos of the camps and Nazi atrocities and a transcript of a radio broadcast made by well known BBC radio news presenter Richard Dimbleby from Bergen-Belsen in May 1945.

The exhibition does not shy away from confronting difficult, complex topics. 'From ancient times' includes information about the 1144 Norwich 'blood libel'; the expulsion of Jews from England in 1290; debates in *The Times* about the credibility of *The Protocols of the Elders of Zion*; and Mosley's British Union of Fascists. British immigration policies, both restrictive and generous, are critically examined. There is material on the 1938 Evian Conference, 1939 White Paper which barred large-scale Jewish migration to Palestine, British post-war immigration policy for Palestine, as well as Britain's pre-war acceptance of over 60,000 Jewish refugees from Nazism (including the *Kindertransporte*) and her post-war welcome of 'the Boys' (orphaned Jewish child survivors).

Although the central story at the IWM focuses on the destruction of the Jews, the suffering of others under Nazism, including homosexuals, the Sinti, Roma and other tribes ('Gypsies'), the fate of physically and mentally disabled people in the T-4 programme, Poles, Soviet POWs, prisoners of conscience and Jehovah's Witnesses are represented as well. The visitor progressing around the exhibition encounters the testimony of others, including a Gypsy, Russian POW and a non-Jewish Polish witness. Moreover, additional information about other victims of Nazism is found on well-placed computer stations. Thus, through an extensive coverage of Nazi racial policy, the exhibition resonates with those in Britain identifying with ethnic and cultural groups persecuted by the Nazis.[83]

Explicit moral lessons are only drawn in the final section of the exhibition, in an audio-visual production entitled 'Reflections', in which some survivors reflect on the meanings of their experiences. Kitty Hart-Moxton hopes that her testimony will serve as a warning for future generations: 'the danger is that whether your are black, whether you are white, whether you are Moslem or Jew, what happened to me could in future happen to you'. The Holocaust is universalized principally through the educational materials that the IWM prepares for the school students who visit the museum. As with those developed by the Museum of Jewish Life, these resource materials suggest ways in which the events of the Holocaust are connected to contemporary political and social contexts in Britain. The Holocaust is connected to the international milieu of genocide though a separate and smaller IWM exhibition, 'Crimes Against Humanity', which through graphic images conveys the horrors of a number of twentieth-century genocides.

A Methodist family, the Smiths, who were adamant that the Holocaust should be a concern for gentiles as well as Jews, as it emerged from Western Christian civilization, established Beth Shalom Holocaust Memorial Centre. Two principles drove their museum project. One, that representations of the Holocaust would reflect the loss, and dignify the memories, of survivors. Two, that 14-year-old students in Britain, with no personal or cultural connection to the Holocaust, should learn about their society and themselves.[84] These principles are reflected throughout the display within which survivor testimony is dispersed and which, where relevant, links the Holocaust to British historical experiences, such as appeasement, the *Kindertransport* and British anti-Semitism.[85] The sufferings of some groups of non-Jewish victims of Nazism are represented but always in relation to the unique fate of European Jewry. 'Jews were the prime focus of the destructive machines and were the group that was singled out for total annihilation.'[86]

Beth Shalom is not only about the past but about the future too. Universal humanistic lessons of the Holocaust are conveyed to visitors through 'Survivors: memories of the past', a video recording of survivors' contemplations of the lessons of the Holocaust which is a permanent feature of the exhibition, and through supplementary educational materials for school students. The Smiths insist that learning from the Holocaust means acting to prevent repetitions of genocide, in any form in any country. Subsequently, they founded the Aegis Institute, which is devoted to genocide prevention.

Representations of the Holocaust at the Leon Greenman, Beth Shalom and IWM museum address both the uniqueness and universality of the Holocaust. Their shared definition of the Holocaust as the Nazis' intended annihilation of European Jewry satisfies the needs of Anglo-Jewry that the memory of Jewish suffering under Nazism be perpetuated for future generations. At the same time, the exhibitions attract the interest of their predominantly non-Jewish audiences by universalizing the Holocaust, either by connecting the destruction of European Jewry to British war experiences, whether of British citizens or British policies and actions, and/or by inviting their audiences to contemplate the lessons of the Holocaust, on an individual, societal and global level.

Even though the IWM is a British institution funded nationally,[87] Beth Shalom a private Christian venture, and the Australian and New Zealand Holocaust museums, as well as the Leon Greenman exhibition, were financed, established and operated predominantly by Jews, their representations of the Holocaust are remarkably similar. By focusing their displays on narrating the Nazis' attempted destruction of European Jewry, the uniqueness of Jewish suffering under Nazism is communicated. Although all museums and exhibitions acknowledge the wider context of Nazi racial policies, only the Imperial War Museum, and Beth Shalom to a lesser degree, provide detailed information about other victims of Nazism, particularly about the fate of the Sinti and Roma (Gypsies), Soviet POWs and the physically and mentally handicapped.

The museums assert that while the principal targets and victims of the Holocaust were Jews, its lessons are universal. All of the museums universalize the Holocaust in one or more ways; differences are only a matter of degree. Though the universal lessons of the Holocaust are rarely conveyed explicitly through the text of the permanent displays, they are a major focus of the educational programmes for school students at the larger museums and exhibitions. Resource materials tackle the implications of the Holocaust for local and national contexts, with Beth Shalom taking a special interest in genocide prevention internationally. While the personal experiences of a British citizen is the major focus of the Leon Greenman exhibition, all of the museums link the Holocaust to the experiences of refugees and survivors who settled and became citizens in the country in which the remembering is taking place.

In short, representations of the Holocaust in these museums communicate shared understandings of the Holocaust and its meanings, despite the museums' divergent sources of origin and the differing national experiences of the countries in which they were established. One can only surmise the reasons for these similarities but any explanation must include not only the perception that Holocaust denial can be countered by educating about the Holocaust, but also the lessons that the Holocaust can convey to multicultural, democratic, Western-orientated societies. Concerns that the universalization of the Holocaust turns attention away from the uniqueness of the Jewish experience under Nazism should be allayed. Indeed, it would appear that the more that the Holocaust is shared with wider society, the greater the likelihood that the uniqueness of Jewish fate under Nazism will not be lost.

Jewish representations of the Holocaust and interpretations of its meanings vary according to the form of public remembrance and the nature of the target audience. The evidence suggests that when Jewish people meet alone to remember the Holocaust, they tend to focus on the uniquely Jewish aspects. In contrast, at Holocaust exhibitions and museums, and at commemorations that are open to the wider community, some universalization of the Holocaust occurs. Likewise, lessons of the Holocaust conveyed to Jews at *Yom haShoah* commemorations have a different emphasis from those conveyed at Holocaust museums that were established predominantly to educate a mass audience about the Holocaust and its meanings. Does this refashioning of the Holocaust and its meanings to suit a particular audience amount to a misuse of the Holocaust? Are there criteria for determining a legitimate reshaping of the Holocaust from a deliberate manipulation? These questions form the basis for the following chapter.

4

Mis(uses) of the Holocaust

There's never been a holiday like this. For £30 you can join the ranks of 40 paying prisoners-of-war at a chillingly realistic Colditz-style concentration camp complete with barbed wire, searchlights, watch towers and 50 guards in SS uniforms. Prisoners arrive in railway cattle trucks late Friday evening, have serial numbers stamped on their foreheads, and spend the rest of the week-end enjoying forced labour, punishing army drills, dowsing with hoses and sleep deprivation.[1]

This advert for an 'adventure holiday' in a mock Nazi concentration camp in Hampshire appeared in a British Tourist Authority guide book in the early 1980s. The concentration camps experience of the Second World War was being commercialized for financial gain. Such distasteful trivialization of the horrors of concentration camp life and of the crimes of the perpetrators attracted complaints that led to the guide book being temporarily withdrawn and amended. Another particularly distorted use of the term 'Holocaust' was made in 1997 by an Australian sports reporter who referred to Iran's World Cup qualifying victory over the Australian soccer team as an 'absolute holocaust'.[2] A more common usage involves adopting the imagery or terminology of the Holocaust to draw attention to, dramatize and increase the impact of a political cause. For example, in 1981 a New Zealand doctor analogized aborted foetuses to Jews killed at Auschwitz. He called on the Jewish community, 'the very people which has suffered most from cruel persecution and attempted extermination over centuries', not to stand by amid 'the current blood bath of antenatal killings being carried out in the country'.[3] In his appeal to stop what he called 'the Holocaust of the innocent', he pointed out that the six million had included 1.5 million children.[4]

How did the term 'Holocaust', which first came into usage in the late 1950s to describe what happened to European Jewry under Nazism, evolve to be used as a metaphor for legalized abortion and a range of societies' 'evils', including AIDS, duck-shooting and the industrialized slaughter of animals for food?[5] For at least thirty years after the end of the Second World War public remembrance of the Holocaust was restricted mainly to Jewish communities. The heroes of the Warsaw Ghetto Uprising and the victims of the Holocaust were mourned at annual commemorations. Yet, in contrast to most other events of the past, the Holocaust did not lose its impact as time moved on. From the late 1970s, representations of the Holocaust, in museums, monuments, books, films and national remembrance days have increased with each passing year. As the events of the Holocaust entered Western consciousness the concept of the Holocaust underwent changes in definition and resonance. The terminology and imagery of the Holocaust were casually, and ever more frequently, used and evoked by those wishing to attract a larger audience to their cause, be it for financial, emotional or political gain. The past decade has even witnessed the exposure of individuals wittingly or unwittingly re-inventing themselves as Holocaust survivors.[6]

Jewish people have responded to these developments with mixed emotions. On the one hand, the status of the Holocaust in Western consciousness as the symbol of the paradigmatic evil, the yardstick against which other massacres is measured, is welcomed. On the other hand, the loose and frequent dilution of the word 'Holocaust' to describe suffering other than the events that overcame European Jewry under Nazism, have caused concern. Many Jews insist that the Holocaust was a unique unparalleled event in history, one that should not be exploited for other political causes. Saba Feniger, Holocaust survivor and retired curator of the Jewish Holocaust Museum & Research Centre (JHM&RC) in Melbourne, speaks for many Holocaust survivors when she explains that she is deeply offended when the Holocaust is carelessly invoked in metaphor: 'the term is used too often and degrades the seriousness of the tragedy that befell us'.[7] Similar sentiments have been expressed in New Zealand, where, as a sociologist of the Jewish community explains, 'the misuse of Holocaust images in the service of anti-Israel or pro-PLO positions by New Zealand cartoonists or writers, or by other activists or individuals, would have caused deeper feelings of distress than any other single act or statement'.[8]

Can we distinguish between invocations of the Holocaust which emanate from sincere conviction and those coming from less laudable motives? Are there happenings in the world that do truly demand comparison to those horrific events? And if there are, what are the criteria to be used for determining that one use of 'Holocaust' is legitimate and another exploitative? This is a question that has vexed Peter

Novick who discussed distinguishing between lessons that have been *drawn from* or *brought to* the Holocaust. Lessons drawn from the Holocaust are those arrived at from reflecting on the Holocaust. Lessons brought to the Holocaust 'reflect values and concerns that originated elsewhere but that seemed to be confirmed by contemplating the Holocaust'.[9] Although this distinction may initially sound apposite, it is, as Novick acknowledged, problematic. In most cases we have no way of ascertaining and measuring the extent to which values and concerns were adhered to previously. Moreover, although the context in which the analogy is invoked would give a pretty good indication, no one can conclusively distinguish which causes are 'authentically connected' to the Holocaust from those that are not. For this reason Novick concluded:

> I don't know of any criterion for the aptness of an analogy except the pragmatic one: does it or doesn't it click? ... Our varying judgments about what are proper and improper lessons of the Holocaust, and what are and aren't appropriate occasions to be reminded of it, depend, in practice, on how we feel about the direction in which those lessons and reminders point. I don't see how it could be otherwise.[10]

Yet Novick's relativism is dangerous in that it can lead to the dilution of the Holocaust. I concur that it is difficult to determine the source of one's motivation for invoking the Holocaust, but contend that we still bear a responsibility to the victims and survivors of the horrific events, as well as to the 'historical truth', to critique, evaluate, respond to and talk about what is acceptable usage and what is not. Examining a variety of invocations of the Holocaust and its imagery, from the general media as well as from Jewish sources, this chapter suggests the adoption of historical accuracy as a criterion for distinguishing between appropriate and inappropriate uses of the Holocaust. While comparisons between the Holocaust and other events either before or since are welcomed, they must be expressed responsibly and ethically, which means that differences as well as similarities must be rigorously elucidated. Comparisons are inappropriate if they only focus on isolated characteristics of complex experiences and events. Historical accuracy must be adopted, both by Jews and non-Jews, as a standard for good practice.

The following three examples from the Australian media illustrate this point. Early in 2002, Dr Michael Dudley of the Royal College of Psychiatry visited Woomera Detention Centre for illegal immigrants to Australia and described conditions as:

barbaric and comparable to a concentration camp ... [the refugees]
are basically locked up in cages and treated like criminals ... Detainees were introduced to us by number, rather than by name ... I'm not
saying it's a death camp; no-one is trying to kill anyone. But the
prologue to what happened in the Holocaust is happening in those
camps.[11]

Dudley was not making a parallel but an analogy. By stating that it was
not a death camp he was alluding to a significant difference – the absence
of an orchestrated policy of annihilation. As he pointed out, there were
no gas chambers, crematoria, torture chambers or planned starvation for
inmates at Woomera.

In contrast, Philip Adams' casual reference to Woomera as a concentration camp in the *Australian* was of a significantly different nature.
Adams didn't compare Woomera to a concentration camp but stated that
it was one.[12] Stan Marks, editor of *Centre News*, the JHM&RC's quarterly
newsletter, found Adams' alleged exploitation of the Holocaust to
promote a political cause 'sickening' and inappropriate.

Of course, Woomera and other similar places should be condemned
and closed right now, but I didn't know that the inmates were being
prepared to be gassed, eliminated completely, had to work from
dawn to dusk, had no medical facilities, slept 50 to a room on hard
bunks with one blanket, were on almost non-existent rations, had
no news from the outside world and so on.[13]

A short time later Adams' weekly column provided a brief history of the
concentration camp, pointing out that the British had used them in the
South African war and Australia had even had concentration camps in
the 1940s for the 'Dunera boys' and other Jewish refugees from Nazism.[14]
However, Adams must have known that his original clumsy use of the
term, without the later information, would draw readers' attention to
compare Woomera with Nazi concentration camps which, in the general
public's mind, erroneously, are synonymous with Nazi death camps.

The difference between Dudley's and Adams' analogies demonstrates the
importance of historical accuracy as a criterion for distinguishing between
proper and improper uses of the terminology and imagery of the Holocaust.
Adams' use served to perpetuate public misperceptions about the different
types of incarceration, instead of contributing to their dissipation.

Other irresponsible uses of Holocaust imagery are found in attempts
by some in the media in Australia, Britain and New Zealand to turn the

Jews, the victims of Nazism, into a reincarnation of the Nazis. For example, a recent cartoon by Michael Leunig depicted a Jew approaching Auschwitz in 1942 with the infamous slogan 'Work Brings Freedom' (*Arbeit Macht Frei*) above the entrance. Juxtapositioned next to it was the same figure approaching an Israeli army barracks with the entrance slogan 'War Brings Peace'. Whether this social commentary is pointing to an equation between the Nazis' Final Solution, symbolized by Auschwitz, with the Sharon government's war on Palestinian terror in the West Bank, or, as Leunig states he intended, as being about 'cruel absurdities, deceptions and fatal ideas',[15] the cartoon was rejected by the *Age* editor, Michael Gawenda, but was reported on by ABC's *Media Watch* programme and posted on their website.[16] While I believe that Leunig is correct to argue that the Holocaust is not beyond comparison, his professional ethics should bind him to making historically accurate comparisons. Intent is the crucial factor here. While Sharon accepts that his government's aim of murdering selected enemy targets will result in some collateral damage to innocent Palestinians, the Nazis aimed at total, systematic annihilation of all Jews; no Jew was to escape the Final Solution. The differences between the Nazis' attempt to exterminate the Jewish people and Sharon's attempt to dismantle the infrastructure which breeds suicide bombers bent on killing innocent civilians are so wide that the comparison is rendered historically invalid.[17] Neither Sharon's words nor deeds indicate an intent to annihilate the Palestinian people. The Nazi regime exterminated six million Jews, that is, two thirds of European Jewry; while there have been less than two thousand victims of Sharon's war on terror in the West Bank.[18] Yet, despite the plain inappropriateness of equating the actions of the Israeli Defence Forces in the West Bank with the genocidal actions of the SS, cartoons similar to Leunig's have appeared in mainstream media in Australia, Britain and New Zealand.[19]

Exploitations of the Holocaust have not been restricted to non-Jews; Jewish people have also used the imagery and terminology of the Holocaust to forward particular agendas. In Israel, those on both sides of the political spectrum have frequently invoked the Holocaust. In May 2003 a poster campaign opposing the 'road map' peace plan depicted rail tracks leading to a swastika, declaring 'Stop the Road Map to Auschwitz'.[20] Has the Holocaust been invoked by Anglo, British and New Zealand Jewish elites to bolster support for, or to deflect criticism from, Israel, as Novick and Finkelstein have suggested has been the case in the US? We saw in the previous chapter that the Zionist lesson has been consistently conveyed at Holocaust commemorations – is this a misuse of Holocaust memory?

My analysis of *Yom haShoah* commemorations reveals that Jews have been concerned about the continued existence of the State of Israel as they remember the Holocaust. However, it would be a mistake to deduce that those expressing the necessity of a Jewish state for Jewish physical survival have been 'playing to the gallery' of prominent non-Jews in the audience in order to bolster gentile support for an increasingly beleaguered Israel. Non-Jews attending the commemorations may have become more supportive of the need for a Jewish state as a result of attending the ceremony and learning about the Holocaust and this would no doubt have pleased the organizers of Holocaust remembrance activities, but in most cases this was not their primary aim. At *Yom haShoah* commemorations in Australia, which have been in the main closed Jewish community affairs, the Zionist lesson is conveyed no less consistently than in Britain where non-Jewish dignitaries are present.[21] Moreover, if the Holocaust was being 'used' as a vehicle for bolstering gentile support for Israel, the Zionist lesson would read loud and clearly at Holocaust museums. This is not the case; although some survivor guides explicitly, and some museum texts implicitly, conveyed the need for a strong Jewish state, this message has not been emphasized as a primary feature in Holocaust museums. References to Israel are few and far between precisely because the museums are fully focused on their primary function of educating the general public about the Holocaust.[22] Guides at the Holocaust Institute of WA in Perth are specifically advised *not* to include the Zionist cause in their narration in order to avoid opening the museum to accusations that it is using the Holocaust to legitimate the policies of the State of Israel.[23]

The Zionist lesson of the Holocaust has resonated with a deeply traumatized post-Holocaust world Jewry.[24] The Holocaust and the establishment and existence of the State of Israel are intricately connected. It has always been an axiom of Zionism that, without a sovereign state, Jews in exile would be vulnerable to persecution and destruction, the Jews would always be victims.[25] In the post-war period, both before and following the establishment of the State of Israel, many survivors in Displaced Persons' Camps settled in the Jewish homeland. Over the past fifty years Jews have escaped anti-Semitism and persecution in various Diaspora communities by settling in Israel. For Jews elsewhere in the Diaspora, the Jewish state continues to serve as a safe haven should the need arise. Yet, while Israel provides security for world Jewry, it has also been under existential threat itself on numerous occasions since its establishment in 1948. This was most clear in the tense days prior to the 1967 Six Day War and in the first days of the Yom Kippur War when

Jews in Israel and the Diaspora feared a second Holocaust. As Dr J. Schneeweiss, President of the Executive Council of Australian Jewry, commented at a commemoration in 1978: 'We faced the all too real threat of a second Holocaust in a single generation ... Memories repressed, but not forgotten, leapt to the forefront again'.[26] This sentiment, and other expressions of solidarity and support for Israel which have been articulated over the years at Holocaust remembrance functions in Australia, Britain and New Zealand, should be understood not as a planned conspiracy by 'Jewish leadership elites' but rather in the context of a post-war world in which anti-Semitism has re-emerged as anti-Zionism and, ironically, in which threats to Israel's existence have been as prevalent as threats to Diaspora Jewry.

Has the Holocaust been invoked by Anglo, British and New Zealand Jewry for other purposes? Assimilation and escalating intermarriage rates, which arguably threaten the survival of the Jewish people, are a major concern shared by Jewish communities worldwide. In the US over 50 per cent of Jews marry non-Jews. In Britain, the intermarriage rate is about 33 per cent and in Australia about 13 per cent.[27] Have Jewish leadership elites promoted the Holocaust in order to increase Jewish identity with the intention that it will serve as a barrier to assimilation?

A common Jewish response to the Holocaust, and one frequently expressed at Holocaust remembrance functions, has been that the destruction of one third of the world's Jewish population, drawn from the great Jewish communities and cultural centres of Europe, called for a re-affirmation of Judaism and a commitment to Jewish cultural life. In London in 1953, Rabbi Rosen declared that the proper way of remembering the 'martyrs' was to remain true to Jewish heritage and to incorporate the courage, faith and spiritual richness of the destroyed communities of Eastern Europe into the lives of the present generation.[28] At the 1962 Auckland commemoration, Rabbi Astor, who frequently through the 1960s read from the Valley of Bones to convey the duty of those who survived to revitalize Jewish knowledge and continuity, provided a practical approach for ensuring Jewish survival.[29]

> There is only one thing we can do, and that is to save as much as possible of the spiritual heritage left to us by our martyred brethren from oblivion ... By living traditional Jewish lives. By continuing our efforts in the rebuilding of Medinat Yisrael [the land of Israel]. By cultivating throughout the Diaspora as well as in our Jewish Homeland a knowledge of the Hebrew language. By enlarging our

tents of learning. By expanding our Jewish schools. By making our Synagogue thrive and flourish and taking an active part in the work of our congregation.[30]

At Sydney's 1968 commemoration, Rabbi Lubofsky, chief minister of St Kilda Synagogue, asserted that 'The Australian Jewish community must not merely survive, but also revive'.[31] Lubofsky urged that Australian Jewry become an heir to the tradition of European Jewry by recreating in Australia all that was lost in Europe.[32]

David Berinson, Youth speaker at Perth's 1990 commemoration, cogently expressed the necessity for a re-dedication to Judaism and Jewish life.

> As Jewish youth, we must realise that the future of the Jewish people rests on our shoulders. It is up to us to take on the responsibility of continuing and enhancing Jewish life by resisting assimilation, affiliating and supporting our communities and Israel, and – above all – by renewing our devotion to Judaism itself.[33]

The context in which these opinions were articulated is crucial. It is both traditional and appropriate at Holocaust remembrance functions to try to make sense of the Holocaust, to draw lessons from and formulate responses to that extreme tragedy. Many Jewish people believe that the construction of a living Jewish people in the present is the most meaningful response to the destruction of the treasures of pre-Holocaust European Jewish culture. These are neither lessons drawn from, or brought to, the Holocaust, but rather responses to it. They aim to ensure Jewish survival in the aftermath of the Holocaust by countering the demographic and spiritual consequences of those terrible events. The speakers cited above urged for a commitment to Jewish observance and identity in response to the Nazis' near destruction of European Jewish culture and traditions, not as a response to assimilation.

Moreover, those few who have blatantly brought the Holocaust to the fight against assimilation have attracted criticism. In Australia, Joshua Henzel's link between and the absence of affordable Jewish education and the subsequent loss of Jewish identity, to 'the quiet Holocaust'[34] prompted some agreement to his overall point, but he was condemned for his use of 'the horrifying expression'.[35] As one critic pointed out: 'The changes in Jewish demography, in the way Jews respond to their origins and traditions, are often worrying. A

"Holocaust" they are not. Because those Jews are alive and we can still do much about it.[36] Likewise, when Eli Sat, *Habonim Shaliach* (Zionist youth envoy from Israel) in NSW, asserted that Jewish assimilation was like 'walking though the gates of another Holocaust … Though assimilation may not be as dramatic as the Holocaust, it is just as severe',[37] his remarks were criticized for being out of context.[38] The use of the term 'a second Holocaust' to describe the results of intermarriage was criticized in Britain too.[39]

Analogies between the Holocaust and assimilation are offensive to many Jews, especially Holocaust survivors. They are also historically irresponsible. The only similarity between the Holocaust and assimilation is their long-term, cumulative effect. The Nazis' systematic annihilation of European Jewry was a serious threat to the continued existence of the Jewish people; wide-scale assimilation could similarly endanger Jewish continuity. If taken to their ultimate conclusions, one would have, and the other could, result in the end of Judaism. In contrast, the short-term effect on the Jewish collective is different, if not the least because the assimilated individual is still alive and can still choose to return to Judaism. The physical destruction and murder of Jews, which was the Holocaust, was irreversible. The most significant dissimilarity is on the individual level. Firstly, the Holocaust was imposed; it was not the free choice of Jews, whereas a decision taken by Jews to abandon their religion and traditions is. Secondly, and most crucially from a moral perspective, death must not be confused with life, even if that life does not continue to be defined as a 'Jewish' one. As one observer in Britain asked in response to a comparison between the Holocaust and intermarriage: 'Has the picture of a Jewish groom and a Gentile bride outside a registry office the same impact … as pictures of Jewish corpses in the snows of Poland?'[40]

Jewish educationalists, religious leaders and scholars in Australia, Britain and New Zealand have for the most part refrained from exploiting the Holocaust as a means of spurious collective identification. Admittedly, this reluctance is not so much a commitment to historical accuracy but to the growing realization that an over-emphasis on Jewish suffering can have a distorting effect on Jewish identity and culture and perhaps even becoming a substitute for Jewish spiritual life, faith and culture as the foundation of 'Jewishness'.[41] British Chief Rabbi Sir Jonathan Sacks contended: 'Unlike traditional Jewish education, Holocaust education in itself offers no meaning, no hope, no way of life'.[42] Indeed, it has been argued that too much focus on the Holocaust, through the proliferation of Holocaust museums and teaching programmes, skews Jewish identity, swamping positive aspects of Jewish life and history, and may even lead to rejection rather than affiliation with a persecuted people.[43] Mill Hill minister Rabbi Yitzhak Schochet went one step further. With one eye on escalating assimilation rates, he criticized what he called 'the Holocaust-obsessed' generation. 'Over a billion dollars has been spent on Holocaust museums while the living are quietly exiting the stage of Jewish history.'[44] In contrast, as David Bryfman, Director of NSW Hillel asserted, a 'healthy' and 'positive' Jewish identity should be based on creating a vibrant Jewish present, a living Jewish people able to carry on the Jewish heritage and transmit its values.

> Jewish identity must be an internal construct and not an external one. We must focus on Jewish culture and not on Nazi persecution as a reason to be Jewish. We must focus on the richness of our religion and not the number of anti-Semitic incidents ... waving Hitler and Auschwitz in the face of our generation will not slow down intermarriage rates. Providing a family environment that encourages the vitality of the Jewish religion, culture, people and all that this entails will significantly lessen the chance of inter-marriage occurring.[45]

Thus, even though assimilation is recognized as a major problem facing world Jewry, the Holocaust has rarely been intentionally promoted to counter that trend as it has been acknowledged that to do so is fraught with complications. Jewish leadership elites would not use the Holocaust to offset assimilation while being aware that it may help solve the problem of Jewish survival but not of Jewish continuity.

While rarely invoked as a tool in the battle against assimilation, the Holocaust has been distorted by Jewish people in other ways. As we shall see in the following examples, the six million Jewish victims of Nazism have frequently been referred to as 'martyrs' who 'sacrificed their lives for the sanctification of God's Holy Name' (*al kiddush hashem*). Martyr-dom is generally defined as encompassing 'those who suffer death rather than renounce religious beliefs'.[46] According to this definition, only those Jews who were given an option of living but chose to die rather than violate their religion, could be considered as martyrs who died '*al kiddush hashem*'. A broader definition of martyr as 'a person who suffers greatly or dies for a cause or belief', would still not include those who died with God's name on their lips if they had no choice but to die.[47] Nevertheless, the myth of the six million martyrs has resonated at Holocaust remembrance functions. The inscription on the United Synagogue's memorial to the Holocaust at Bushey Cemetery in Britain reads:

> In everlasting memory of the martyrdom of the holy communities and of the six million Jews cruelly slaughtered for the sanctification of the Name during the Holocaust.[48]

Similarly, at Auckland's 1962 commemoration, Rabbi Astor referred to the 'six million martyred brethren' who died *'al kiddush hashem'*. He pointed out that 'they came from many lands, from the deep of the seven seas, from the ends, and ravines of Europe, from the lethal chambers and slaughterhouses of the concentration camps and ghettoes'.[49] Yet, Astor failed to acknowledge that they also came from a wide variety of Jewish backgrounds: not all, or even most, were Orthodox. Among the six million were Reform Jews, Bundists, secular Jews, atheists, assimilated, non-practising Jews as well as baptized converts.[50] To relate to these converts, as well as to assimilated and secular Jews, as martyrs who died *'al kiddush hashem'* falsifies their lives and deaths. They did not have a choice. If the option had been presented, it is likely that many would have denounced Judaism in order to live.

The Warsaw Ghetto Uprising has frequently been linked to the idea of martyrdom and *al kiddush hashem*. At London's 1956 commemoration, Dayan M. Steinberg asserted that 'the Warsaw Ghetto Rising was the supreme expression of *kiddush hashem*'.[51] This misappropriation is a flagrant desecration of the truth. Many of the leaders of the Warsaw Ghetto Uprising, as well as many of the participants, were from *Hashomer Hatzair*, a socialist, secular Zionist youth movement. They did not choose to die in the name of a god they did not believe in. If they were 'martyrs' it was in the name of freedom, but even this is difficult to argue because their choice was not really about whether to live or die, but about how to die – fighting in self-defence and with honour in freedom, or passively, without resistance in captivity.

In all of the cases cited above, the identities of the six million Jewish victims of Nazism were being refashioned as observant Jews. This myth provides moral authority for the Orthodox establishment to interpret the lessons of the Holocaust on their behalf. Have Orthodox establishments disseminated this falsehood to bolster their authority? While the roots of the myth of the six million 'martyrs' can only be surmised, there is no uncertainty as to its successful promulgation amongst world Jewry. An editorial in *Centre News*, the newsletter of the Jewish Holocaust Museum and Research Centre in Melbourne, urges the importance of gathering and recording names and photographs of members of survivors' families so they can be kept for posterity 'to find and learn about their existence and their martyrology'.[52] The newsletter's editor, Cyla Sokolowicz, and many of those who founded the museum, were secular Bundists,[53] yet they, too, have adopted the terminology of this traditional way of confronting death and tragedies in Jewish history without thinking critically about its meanings and implications. Perhaps the widespread association of the Jewish victims of Nazism with martyrdom should not be surprising. *Yom haShoah* has been referred to in official commemoration programmes and newspaper articles as 'Martyrs Memorial Day' for most of the post-war period and the full name of *Yad Vashem*,[54] established in Jerusalem in 1953, is *Yad Vashem* Holocaust Martyrs' and Heroes Memorial Authority.[55]

Not only is the usage of 'martyr' historically invalid but it also, by implication, reflects negatively on those who were prepared to relinquish their cause for the chance of life, or those who died without a cause, as indeed was the experience of the vast majority of the six million Jewish victims of Nazism. This myth should be challenged and rectified and a new definition of Jewish martyrdom in the Holocaust embraced. The appellation of martyr should refer to those Jews who had a choice not to die but chose to sacrifice their own lives, or suffer greatly, for a cause. This would encompass, among others, those partisans who died sabotaging Nazi war efforts or Nazi attempts to carry out the Final Solution. Included, too, would be Arthur Zygelbiom, Jewish Bundist member of the Polish Free Government in London, who committed suicide to draw attention to the fate of the Jews of Poland. Zygelbiom can be regarded as a martyr as he had a choice and chose to die for a cause. Similarly, Janusz Korczak would fall under this category as he had the option of escaping from the Warsaw Ghetto to the Aryan side but would not leave without the children from the orphanage he directed. Korczak was consequently deported and gassed at Treblinka with the children.

As the Holocaust became an element in the consciousness of Western societies from the mid-1970s, its imagery and terminology entered popular usage. Jews in Australia, Britain and New Zealand, irrespective of the size and composition of their communities, have been extremely sensitive to the Holocaust being carelessly invoked in metaphor, and to any events being compared to the Holocaust, for fear that the result will be the relativisation of Jewish suffering. Yet, as we have seen, Jewish people themselves, like other peoples, have not been immune from misappropriating their own history. This chapter argues that those who invoke Holocaust terminology and imagery, Jewish or otherwise, must do so responsibly. They must not only display an awareness of the sensitivities of Holocaust survivors and their descendants, but also a commitment to historical accuracy. In this way, the singularity and enormity of the Holocaust will be preserved while keeping it relevant for humankind.

5

Holocaust Memorialization and Jewish (Dis)unity

Do collective acts of remembrance unite those participating, or are commemorations and anniversaries characterized by struggles for control over the event being remembered and its significance? Much of the recent literature conceptualizes collective memory as a disputed terrain. David Thelen maintains that 'struggles over the possession and inter-pretation. of memories are deep, frequent, and bitter'.[1] Paula Hamilton has asserted that 'Reunions and anniversaries are often the forums for bitter debate between participants about the memory of an event, even when they were all witnesses to it. They argue over what happened and what interpretation to place on the experience.'[2] John Gillis has em-phasized the authoritarian and undemocratic nature of commemorations that construct and control an official history of past events. Gillis, like Thelen, holds that commemorations may appear consensual but they are 'the product of processes of intense contest, struggle, and, in some instances, annihilation'.[3] In contrast, one of the underlying assumptions of Peter Novick's *The Holocaust in American Life* is that Holocaust com-memorations tend to unify those doing the remembering.[4]

Indeed, on the surface, Novick appears to be correct. A common pattern of Holocaust memorialization has developed in Jewish comm-unities worldwide and, at first glance, these collective acts of Holocaust remembrance look as if they unite world Jewry. *Yom haShoah* and other Holocaust commemorations are derived from Jewish tradition and culture. The memorial day, which inscribes memory of an event into the Jewish calendar, is a traditional Jewish response to catastrophe.[5] Histor-ical memory has consistently been central to Jewish identity and survival. Lucette Valenci reminds us:

> With their dispersal, the Jews became a people of memory. To be Jewish is to remember. Jewish existence is moulded, not by theo-logy, but by the ritualization of history, by recalling untiringly the events of the past.[6]

Similarly, Yosef Hayim Yerushalmi argues that, 'Only in Israel and nowhere else is the injunction to remember felt as a religious imperative to an entire people'.[7] Israeli Holocaust remembrance practices and the World Jewish Congress' occasional recommendations about commemorations further serve to homogenize Holocaust memorialization in the Diaspora.[8]

Not only the form, but also the rituals and symbols of *Yom haShoah* commemorations are rooted in Jewish tradition. The annual Holocaust commemorations have acquired a familiar set of core rituals over the years, including a minute's silence in memory of the victims of the Holocaust; the ceremonious lighting by survivors or their families of six *Yahrzeit* candles, symbolizing the six million Jews murdered by the Nazis; and the simple but solemn memorial service including the recitation of the prayers *El Mole Rachamim* and *Kadish.*[9] Following the speeches and artistic presentations (which regularly include the singing of *'Ani Ma'amin'*, the hymn of unvanquished Jewish hope and faith, and the Partisan Song, the hymn of the Jewish resistance in Poland, the ceremony generally ends with the *Hatikvah*, the Israeli national anthem.[10]

Furthermore, as we have already seen in chapter three, the focus of Holocaust commemorations, and understandings and interpretations of the meanings of the Holocaust, have evolved in similar ways across the Jewish Diaspora. Superficially then, it would appear that the annual gatherings of Jews collectively to remember the Holocaust and mourn its victims have been characterized by uniformity and consensus. Have the forces of Jewish tradition and culture overridden other aspects of difference within and between Jewish communities? Has Holocaust memorialization really been consensual despite the diverse composition of Jewish communities? Further, did not the dominant cultures in the country in which the remembering was taking place produce diverse approaches to Holocaust memorialization?

The following analysis of selected episodes of Holocaust memorialization in Australia, Britain and New Zealand sheds light on an ambiguous relationship between remembrance of the Holocaust and Jewish unity. Tensions between the forces pushing for Jewish unity and uniformity, and the reality of the existence of diversity within and between the communities are demonstrated through case studies of three sites of disunity. Conflicts over various aspects of the annual *Yom haShoah* commemorations; heated debates over the institution of an annual Holocaust Memorial Day in London; and the animosity surrounding participation in Holocaust commemorations in Poland demonstrate the complexities of the commemorative process and offer broader observations about the study of collective memory.

YOM HASHOAH COMMEMORATIONS

The wish of the Orthodox rabbinate to maintain its hold over Jewish communities, and the demand of the Liberal rabbinate to have a voice in public functions which would be equal to their growing following, have been evident across the Diaspora. In Wellington, Perth and Sydney, this deep-seated conflict between Orthodox and Reform strands of Judaism spilled over into *Yom haShoah* commemorations and led not only to decreased attendance but also posed a major threat to the fundamental design of holding united *Yom haShoah* commemorations.[11]

According to Anne Beaglehole and Hal Levine's study of Jewish life in New Zealand, 'cooperation and common ground between the [Orthodox and Liberal] congregations exists alongside bitterness, antagonism and conflict'.[12] Holocaust memorialization is one area that has witnessed both cooperation and conflict.[13] Whereas the Orthodox and Liberal communities in Wellington worked together to contribute towards the success of the aforementioned 1985 commemoration, some members of the Orthodox community did not respond favourably to the arrangement, implemented in the 1990s, that the annual *Yom haShoah* commemorations would take place in Reform and Orthodox synagogues in alternate years.[14] Most of the Reform congregation attend the commemorations at the Orthodox synagogue but every second year, when the Reform congregation deem it their turn to host the annual function, some Orthodox leaders and members refuse to attend,[15] preferring to say the prayers appropriate to *Yom haShoah* in their own synagogue. They do this as they do not recognize Reform synagogues as places of worship and do not want to be seen to be supporting Reform Judaism.[16] Thus, for the past decade, every second year on *Yom haShoah* there has been antagonism between the two congregations in Wellington.

These conflicts not only caused ill-feeling between the two congregations but also had a negative effect on those, mostly Holocaust survivors, who organized the annual commemorations. One survivor said that she was annoyed to think that Orthodox Jews, including Rabbis, would attend a service in a Church but not in a Reform synagogue, adding: 'it is "painful" that those making the decisions are so negative … its degrading, unbelievable that they can act in this way'.[17] Another survivor, a member of the Orthodox congregation herself, asked: 'How can the Orthodox Rabbi influence the young people not to go there, our own people … it's disgusting and narrow minded'.[18] Her British-born husband added that in these circumstances he would not be surprised if survivors would not want anything to do with the community.[19] Another survivor stated: 'I don't want to be involved; usually there are problems with the Orthodox and the Temple and I get annoyed and upset with intolerance'.[20] Indeed, one Holocaust survivor, who plays a central role in organizing the annual commemorations and has increasingly come to perceive this task as an 'incredible hassle', dreaded the impending 2003 commemoration which the Reform congregation considered it their turn to host. He stated: 'there could be conflict – if there is anyone left who cares enough!'[21]

In Britain and Australia, the overriding aim of making *Yom haShoah* commemorations inclusive of all sections of the Jewish community led to the main memorial evening taking place in 'neutral' venues – a civic setting or a Jewish communal centre at which all could attend, irrespective of religious or political identification.[22] Synagogues were generally ruled out as appropriate venues, despite the compelling financial advantages, in order to avoid potential conflict between the adherents of the two antithetical strands of Judaism.

Yet, while Wellington Jewry was divided over the appropriate venue for the annual commemorations, the Liberal and Orthodox congregations in Sydney and Perth clashed over the performance of the rituals. Even though many members of Sydney's substantial Liberal community had lost family in the Holocaust, the Minister of Temple Emanuel, Sydney's Liberal congregation, was not invited to participate in the unveiling and consecration of the Martyrs' Memorial Monument at Rookwood cemetery in 1970. Temple President Dr Victor Bear pointed out that the spiritual leadership of the two major congregational bodies in Sydney should be present, as the Nazis had not differentiated between Liberal and Orthodox Jews. Temple chief minister, Rabbi Dr R. Brasch, asserted 'The shortsightedness and narrowmindedness thus expressed makes something which should have been a hallowed occasion, not a consecration but a desecration'.[23] Dr H. Wachtell, chairman of the Overseas Jewry and Communal Integration Committee of the NSW Board of Deputies, said the project should be a unified memorial, 'An expression of this Board is needed to save the community from splitting unnecessarily'.[24] Many members of the NSW Board of Deputies criticized the omission of the Liberals, and the Board officially expressed its concern to the two organizing bodies, Sydney's *Chevra Kadisha* and the Cemetery Trust, but to no avail; no Liberal minister or Temple executive was invited to attend the ceremony in honour of the six million Jewish victims of Nazism.[25] Rabbi Dr R. Brasch described the omission of the Liberals from the function as a 'terrible blow' to communal unity. 'Only a feeling of deep shame and frustration can be the result.'[26] This was not the last clash in Sydney between Liberal and Orthodox over Holocaust remembrance.

The NSW Board of Deputies' occasional invites to Liberal Reverend Cantor Michael Deutsch, a Hungarian Holocaust survivor, to recite *Kadish* at *Yom haShoah* commemorations, led to Orthodox Rabbis boycotting the functions in the late 1970s and early 1980s.[27] The Orthodox leadership reiterated the long-standing *halachic* ruling (according to Jewish law, custom and tradition), held universally by Orthodox rabbinical authorities, that Orthodox Rabbis cannot and will not participate in public prayer with their Liberal counterparts. The Board executive attempted to find a solution to the conflict between Orthodox and Liberal Jewry on this issue, but 'No such agreement was forthcoming because the Board was not prepared to accept the uncompromising position advanced by the Association of Jewish Ministers'.[28] Leslie Caplan, President of the NSW Jewish Board of Deputies, expressed the sentiments of the Board and probably the majority of Sydney Jewry when he declared that the whole Jewish community should be united together on *Yom haShoah*: 'We wish as a collective act to remember what has been done to us collectively'.[29] The problem flared up publicly again in 1994, when an invite was offered again to Deutsch to officiate at the fiftieth anniversary commemoration of the destruction of Hungarian Jewry. Orthodox Rabbis boycotted the function.[30] The Orthodox rabbinate's priority, religious principles over Jewish community unity, was clearly stated by the President of the Rabbinical Council of New South Wales, Rabbi Selwyn Franklin, who decried what he understood to be the Board's attempt 'to encourage the rabbinate to forsake fundamental Torah values in order to promote the Board's perception of communal harmony'.[31] Unless invited to officiate, relatively few Orthodox Rabbis have attended the main community *Yom haShoah* commemorations.[32]

A similar conflict occurred in Perth where the Liberals demanded the right for a Liberal Rabbi to stand shoulder to shoulder with the Orthodox Rabbi to recite the *Kadish* prayer at the annual Warsaw Ghetto Commemorations. The Orthodox leadership refused to participate in public prayer with their Liberal counterparts. The conflict between the Liberal and Orthodox leadership was finally resolved by a WA Board of Deputies declaration that, in future, while religious services may be held at both the Perth Hebrew Congregation and Temple David, the annual Holocaust commemoration would be a lay meeting.[33] Since 1972 the religious ceremony has been performed by lay leaders and not by Rabbis. Consequently, although the religious content of the commemoration remained unchanged, the overall involvement of Rabbis in the commemoration decreased. The animosity between Liberal and Orthodox led to increased secularization of Perth Jewry's *Yom haShoah* function. Melbourne's Jewish community was spared this kind of disunity because the Liberal leadership chose not to challenge the Orthodox hegemony over the main community *Yom haShoah* commemorations, and the Jewish Heritage Committee of the Victorian Jewish Board of Deputies did not disturb the *status quo* by inviting Liberal clergy to lead the prayers.[34]

Ironically, the commemoration of the Warsaw Ghetto fighters, who put aside their differences of politics and of sectarian religion to wage a united armed struggle against the Nazis, provided an occasion for the divisive struggle between Liberal and Orthodox Jewry in Wellington, Sydney and Perth.

Yom haShoah commemorations in London also failed to unite Anglo-Jewry despite the best efforts of Ben Helfgott, Holocaust survivor and Chairman of the Yad Vashem Committee UK (YVCUK) from 1986, to bring Anglo-Jewry together in collective remembrance and mourning of the Jewish victims of Nazism. Helfgott made substantial efforts to attract a large audience to the 1986 *Yom haShoah* commemoration at the Holocaust monument at Hyde Park.[35] The YVCUK wrote to Rabbis requesting that they devote sermons to the Holocaust on the *Shabbat* before *Yom haShoah*, and to headmasters of all Jewish schools, to youth groups and to the Union of Jewish Students to arrange programmes for *Yom haShoah*.[36] A *Jewish Chronicle* editorial supported the effort and encouraged British Jewry 'who have shied away until now from embracing so detailed a national memorial ... to take *Yom Hashoah* firmly into our communal calendar'.[37] Helfgott, who had hoped for a 10,000 turnout,[38] was naturally disappointed in 1986 when sixty-three people turned up, including only seven communal leaders and a handful of youth.[39] The words of one survivor surely reflected the feelings of Helfgott and the YVCUK: 'what happened in Hyde Park last week was, as it were, a public desecration, which mocks the dead and shames the living!'[40] Nevertheless, the YVCUK persisted. The President of the Board was invited to be the main speaker at the 1987 commemoration at the Hyde Park Memorial. The strategies of the previous year were repeated and further intensified. As a result of the intensive campaign, between 2,000–3,000 people were present at the 1987 commemoration.[41] Although attendance was much higher than in previous years, Helfgott was not satisfied. He criticized the attitude of a number of the Rabbis to the event: 'Some of them didn't inform their congregants; urge them to come, or come themselves'.[42] In 1989 a meeting was to be arranged with the Chief Rabbi 'to try and engage more commitment from him and from the United Synagogues'.[43] After an attendance of only 1,000 at the 1989 commemoration, Helfgott vowed to continue trying to persuade community leaders to take the event more seriously.[44] Helfgott eventually had a breakthrough with regard to the religious establishment which, after almost half a century of inactivity in the area of Holocaust remembrance, became relatively more supportive. In 1992 the Chief Rabbi Jonathan Sacks designated the day before the Holocaust commemoration at Hyde Park as *Shabbat Shoah*[45] and personally led the memorial service alongside the charismatic and widely respected Reform Rabbi and Auschwitz survivor, Hugo Gryn. Yet success was still limited – only 500 attended the rain-drenched ceremony. Survivor Sam Pivnick declared 'It's a pity we are so few … Everybody should be here, whether they are young or old, it doesn't matter. But people always find excuses.'[46]

While some were put off attending by the aesthetics of the monument,[47] others complained about the format and organization of the function. The arrangements whereby those participating in the ceremony and other dignitaries, referred to sarcastically as 'royalty', were sectioned off into a more spacious 'privileged' area was resented. One survivor was offended that she had received an invitation to attend the ceremony, but had been forced by stewards to stand outside of the enclosure where the ceremony was while Board members and their wives were given 'pride of place'.[48] Beyond these problems there were also seating, transport and parking problems associated with the advanced age of many of those attending.[49] In 1993 a *Jewish Chronicle* editorial commented:

> [The memorial] has been marred, however, by the paucity of numbers attending – usually barely a couple of hundred, and most of them elderly. It has failed to attract the youth, save for the occasional Jewish school party brought along by enlightened teachers. Nor is it only the youth who are missing. Precious few lay or religious communal figures, educationalists, fund-raisers, academics or cultural figures are seen gathering round the stark stone memorial in the heart of London.[50]

Such a statement brings into sharp relief that assumptions such as those made by Novick, about Holocaust memorialization generating increased Jewish community unity, cannot be supported. Sadly, the aforementioned examples demonstrate that Holocaust commemorations have also generated significant disappointment, frustration and resentment in Jewish communities.

HOLOCAUST MEMORIAL DAY IN BRITAIN

The 1990s witnessed a vast increase in Holocaust remembrance activities in Britain. While some British Jews were working towards raising Holocaust consciousness in mainstream British culture, others were feeling uncomfortable with its prominence. Nowhere were these divisions clearer than in the debate about the appropriateness of institutionalizing an annual Holocaust Memorial Day in Britain's national calendar. From its suggestion until fruition there was no clear consensus on the proposal for a Holocaust Memorial Day.

Those supporting the idea argued that after the demise of the survivors, the Holocaust would be in danger of being relegated to a minor event in history. A nationally observed Holocaust Memorial Day would ensure remembrance of the events that overcame European Jewry between 1933 and 1945.[51] One survivor stated:

> The memorial day is a wonderful thing. We can honour the murdered and mark the inhumanity shown to us. We can grieve for each other. For those who were downgraded and excluded, to be given this national recognition is in total opposition to what the Nazis had planned for us.[52]

The initiative was generally supported by Jewish leaders, some of whom were included on the Working Group which was under the aegis of the Home Office which had initiated the original consultation paper in 1999. The President of the Board of Deputies, Eldred Tabachnik QC, asserted:

> The tragedies we have seen throughout the world since World War Two remind us of the need for eternal vigilance and commitment to learn the lessons of the past. Britain can be proud of the lead it takes in combating racism and in promoting an open society. I believe the Government's proposals will build on this and ensure that generations to come understand the importance of the past for their future.[53]

The Jewish Orthodox establishment had been expressing unease about the dominant position of the Holocaust in Jewish identity since 1988 when former British Chief Rabbi, Lord Immanuel Jakobovits, first warned against the dangers of grounding Jewish identity on a history of tragedies: '[Jews] must beware against nurturing and breeding a Holocaust mentality of morose despondency among our people, especially our youth'.[54] This line of thinking was also expressed by Orthodox Rabbi Yitzhak Shochet, of London's Mill Hill Synagogue, who asserted that Jews should focus more on the present, on what it means to be Jewish today.[55] It was argued that over-emphasis on the Holocaust, on the Jews as victims, conveys an unbalanced portrait of Jews, for non-Jews and Jews alike. Yet these anxieties about the central place of the Holocaust in Jewish culture and identity did not necessarily lead to Jewish religious opposition to the proposal for a nationally observed Holocaust Memorial Day. Jonathan Sacks recognized the positive in the idea by declaring that: 'The day will be a powerful reminder of the vulnerability and necessity of freedom and the dignity of difference'.[56] Rabbi Tony Bayfield, chief executive of the Reform Synagogues of Great Britain, said a remembrance day would be 'a timely move that would both reflect one of the great tragedies of the 20th century and acknowledge the multi-religious character of Britain today'.[57]

However, unease with the proposal was expressed from a variety of Jewish sources.[58] One survivor explained:

> it is painful to those of us who have suffered human loss in the camps to have the wound constantly probed. Who, in any case, are those self-appointed spokesmen who purport to act on our behalf?[59]

Also, there was concern that the day would be ignored by large sections of the population, causing distress to survivors.

> I and quite a lot of my friends who grieve daily for our loved ones who perished in the camps, feel very strongly against an enforced, organised memorial day. The world must never forget what happened ... [but] Please, no set date in England, it would back-fire and hurt![60]

By 'backfire and hurt' the author is probably expressing the fear that the institution of such a day could cause resentment from others who have suffered but have no set remembrance day, and could possibly even lead to acts of terror and/or desecration from extreme anti-Semites. On a similar plane, Rabbi Dr Jonathan Romain, minister of the Maidenhead Reform synagogue and the son of a Holocaust survivor argued 'if it is greeted by apathy by the public at large, the message of indifference will be counter-productive and encourage revisionists to peddle their lies more openly'.[61] Furthermore, it was pointed out that remembering on one specific day may relieve the community of the burden of memory for the rest of year which could paradoxically distance the Holocaust from British life and culture.[62]

These concerns were compounded by what were perceived as the questionable motives of the Blair government. There was disquiet that politicians would devise a narrative of the Holocaust that would end with a celebration of British moral supremacy.[63] It was feared that awkward questions would be avoided, such as past and contemporary British links with countries with human rights abuses, as well as British policies restricting Jewish immigration to Palestine.[64] Taking the line of government exploitation and politicization one step further, *JC* columnist Norman Lebrecht cynically declared the day as: 'an abomination, a desecration of the dead ... a pair of peak time-chasing politicians ... [making] a media event out of the martyrdom, as a mockery of memory'. Moreover, Lebrecht argued that others will demand that their Holocausts be remembered too but

> Any comparison to other massacres desecrates the dead ... Without an acknowledgment that the Christian world was at fault in its attitude towards Jews, uniquely and unequivocally at fault, any commemoration is hollow. Without giving absolute priority to the claims of survivors, any Holocaust Day would be an insult to the dead.[65]

Simon Sebag-Montefiore was even more scathing in his cynicism:

> This is meant to be about the death of millions of innocent people but it sounds as if, to the Government, 27 January is really New Labour's Anti-Racist PC Catch-all Panaceas Day, meant to advertise Mr Blair's 'clear vision', a chilling phrase in its own right.[66]

The divisions amongst Anglo-Jewry became more pronounced when opposition was expressed to the singling out of the Holocaust among other twentieth-century atrocities. An 'International Genocide Day', which would focus not only on the victims of the Holocaust but also on survivors of other twentieth-century genocides and atrocities, was preferred. Ed Kessler, executive director of the Centre for Jewish–Christian Relations in Cambridge, asserted that, 'The day should also be used to highlight the genocides that have continued since the Holocaust – and which still continue today'.[67] Similarly, Rabbi Dr Jonathan Romain favoured a 'Victims' Day' that would commemorate all who have suffered dictatorship or discrimination.[68] He feared that the current proposal 'has led many to accuse Jews of being concerned only with their own history and being insensitive to the sufferings of others'.[69] Jewish educationalist Ronnie Landau argued that the suffering of the Palestinians and the victims of other tragedies should be remembered together with the Holocaust.[70] This approach to Holocaust remembrance has offended other Anglo-Jews who feel that any comparison to other genocides desecrates the Jewish victims of Nazism.

Whereas the previous year there had been another poor attendance at the *Yom haShoah* function, there were not enough seats to meet Jewish community demands at the inaugural Holocaust Memorial Day ceremony on 27 January 2001. The high profile of the event and its extensive coverage by the British media had made remembrance of the Holocaust of major importance for many Jews who had previously been disinterested. Yet this increased Jewish attraction to Holocaust remembrance also led to animosities. Jewish leaders fought over the seating arrangements – to be nearer to the dignitaries and perhaps, to catch a glimpse of themselves on national TV.[71] The President of the Board of Deputies, Jo Wagerman, had been seated in isolation from the main representatives of the Jewish community and was not invited to join the group who met the Prince of Wales and the Prime Minister. Wagerman complained that 'Others seated nearer the centre included the husband of the woman who had trained one of the choirs, and two rabbis from the North London Progressive Synagogue, who ... were there because they were married to each other'.[72]

There was no unified Anglo-Jewish response to the proposal for the institution of a Holocaust Memorial Day and Jews in Britain remain divided over the benefits of its continued existence. Tensions in the Jewish community have not abated despite the outward 'success' of the high-profile inaugural Holocaust Memorial Day. In an article in the *Jewish Chronicle*, historian Geoffrey Alderman asserted:

> As for Holocaust Memorial Day, show me the British Jew who thinks this is a good idea, and I will show you a fool. We Anglo-Jews do not need to be reminded of the Holocaust. Nor – in my experience – do our many gentile friends in these islands. Our many gentile enemies will only exploit the event in order to discomfort us. I have already heard calls for the event to include the self-inflicted Palestinian Arab 'holocaust' of 1948–9.[73]

The idea that Anglo-Jews do not need reminding of the Holocaust is totally baffling, but the crux of Alderman's concern is in his second point. Here, Alderman has got it right. There *is* a real fear among British Jews, even more so since the pro-Palestinian media coverage of the second *intifada*, that organizers of future national Holocaust Memorial Day commemorations may choose to address the issue of the alleged 'Palestinian holocaust'. This really would be a case of the whole idea 'backfiring' as suggested by one survivor earlier. In the future, ironically perhaps, Anglo-Jewry may find itself uniting in an effort to confront that very challenge.

'HOLOCAUST TOURISM' TO POLAND

Since the end of the Second World War it has been common among Jewish refugees from Nazi-occupied Europe to return to visit their former or ancestral 'homes', the 'Old World'. They generally pay homage to their deceased ancestors by visiting both the places from which they or their families originated and the sites of destruction at which family members and friends perished, or in some cases, endured and survived, during the Nazi era. It is hoped by survivors that these 'pilgrimages' will help them to reconcile themselves with their nightmarish pasts and also that as an outcome of the shared experience, their children may be motivated to take over the legacy of remembering the Holocaust.[74] Whereas these private, individual or small family explorations of personal pasts have evoked few negative responses, organized delegations to commemorations in Warsaw, or organized tours to concentration camps and death camps in Poland, which comprise the vast majority of Jews who travel to Poland,[75] have on occasion caused major divisions within some communities.

In 1983 the increasingly anti-Semitic nature of the communist Polish regime led Britain's Polish Jewish Ex-Servicemen's Association (PJEX) to appeal to Anglo-Jewry to break with tradition and not send a delegation to Warsaw for the fortieth anniversary commemoration of the Warsaw Ghetto Uprising.[76] A member of the PJEX slammed the proposed delegation as a 'shameful mission … the Poles are arranging this circus only for the purpose of getting dollars'.[77] The PJEX's stance caused such controversy and animosity between certain individuals and organizations that for a while the crisis threatened the tradition of holding one, united Holocaust commemoration in London.[78]

The PJEX's campaign was to no avail; the Board of Deputies of British Jews voted overwhelmingly in favour of participating.[79] Most Jewish community organizations were not in agreement with the PJEX's standpoint. Indeed, the 45 Aid Society of Holocaust Survivors and the Association of Jews of Polish Origin, many of whose members had suffered in Poland, sent delegates to Warsaw.[80] Those in favour of British participation in the commemorations in Warsaw pointed out that they were not in disagreement with the PJEX's interpretation of the nature of the Polish regime. However, they contended that the delegation to Warsaw would be a pilgrimage to honour the dead and to support the tiny remnant of Jews in Poland. In addition, it was argued that participation would lead to public debate in Poland, a communist state, about its relationship with Israel and world Jewry, and about anti-Semitism within its borders. Further, it was claimed that by attending the commemorations in Warsaw, Jews would reassert and reclaim Jewish resistance and Jewish martyrdom which were being obscured by official Polish historiography and the organisers of the commemorative event.[81]

The debate further intensified and reached a level of serious conflict after the vice-chairman of the Board's Foreign Affairs Committee (who was also chairman of the Warsaw Ghetto Memorial organizing com-mittee), circulated a letter to all sponsoring organisations criticising the speech made by Simon Frisner, President of the PJEX, at the 1983 commemoration.[82] Frisner's opposition to the sending of a delegation to Poland was perceived as 'an implicit attack on the Board' and to all who had attended the commemoration in Poland.[83] Most controversially, it was suggested that the Warsaw Ghetto Memorial organizing committee reconsider the Chairmanship of the commemoration meeting. Members of the PJEX were aghast and explained to the Board's President that the organization of the Warsaw Ghetto Memorial is 'our committee, created by us ... and all other organizations are sponsoring organizations'.[84] Moreover, the PJEX emphasized that the Holocaust was their tragedy: 'others come to share the sorrow, but we are the nearest and most affected ones'.[85] Furthermore, it was argued that:

> The facts concerning the Christian population in Poland before and after the war and the atrocities committed by the Germans with the help of the local population are well known and as former residents in Poland we have every right to express what we feel about our former co-residents. We still have it in our minds, because we and our friends experienced all forms of Polish antisemitism and huliganism [*sic*] ... we have the right to express it during the Warsaw Ghetto commemoration meeting.[86]

The PJEX demanded that the author of the letter resign or be removed from his position as Chairman of the Warsaw Ghetto Memorial organizing committee and be replaced by the President of the Board.[87]

However, Greville Janner, President of the Board, stood firm behind his colleague and for a while separate Holocaust commemorations, one for the PJEX and another for the Board and its supporters, seemed the only way forward.[88] Eventually, a compromise, which was far from a victory for the PJEX, determined that the Chairman of the organizing committee should be whoever the Board's Foreign Affairs committee nominates, and that the Chairman of the PJEX would continue to be the Chairman of the memorial meeting but 'it being clearly understood that his task is to introduce the subject and the speakers briefly and without introducing contentious views'.[89]

What considerations motivated the Board's decisions in this matter? There are a number of possibilities. In the opinion of the Board's representatives, the PJEX's insistence on focusing on the Warsaw Ghetto Uprising was a barrier to increased attendance at the annual functions. Is this incident best understood in the context of the Board's attempts to maintain control over Jewish communal life? Was the Board attempting to calm the dissenting voice of the PJEX in order to maintain an appearance of Anglo-Jewish unity? These explanations would fit in with Yael Zerubavel's contention that 'The commemoration of historical events is not only a powerful means of reinforcing social solidarity but also an arena of struggle over power and control'.[90] Anglo-Jewish–Polish relations were an additional political concern determining the Board's decision-making in the area of Holocaust commemorations. Was the Board attempting to avoid a direct conflict with the Poles over 'who owns Auschwitz'?

Whatever the motivations, the whole affair makes one question whether what has appeared to be shared Anglo-Jewish understandings of the Holocaust and its meanings, actually reflected reality. Perhaps other 'unpopular', minority or contentious memories of the Holocaust which express histories of past events which contradict the official version have been passed over for the sake of the appearance of unity. Anglo-Jewish 'unity', observed through the collective participation in rituals and mourning, only thinly veils the kind of intense struggles for memory that Gillis, Thelen and others have written about. In other words, Anglo-Jewish unity surrounding Holocaust remembrance may be no more than an illusion.

The sending of delegations to Warsaw for the annual commemoration of the Warsaw Ghetto uprising comprises only one aspect of organized Jewish tourism to Poland. The most widely attended and high-profile tour to Poland is the March of the Living (MOTL) that was instituted in 1988, organized by the United Israel Appeal (UIA). This is a two-week educational study tour that includes a week in Poland and a week in Israel. Participants visit historic Jewish sites such as Cracow and Lublin as well as the sites of destruction, including the Warsaw Ghetto Memorial, Maijdanek and Treblinka. On *Yom haShoah* Jews from all over the world join together to march the three-kilometre route from the concentration camp at Auschwitz to the gas chambers at Birkenau, retracing the steps taken by hundreds of thousands of Jews before they were murdered by the Nazis. The second half of the programme takes place in Israel where the students participate in a study programme at *Yad Vashem*, tour the country, commemorate *Yom haZikaron* (Israel's Day of Remembrance for fallen soldiers) and celebrate *Yom ha'Atzmaut* (Israel's Independence Day). Thus participants explore the depths of despair in Poland and the heights of redemption in Israel.

Australian participation in organized tours to Poland, whether in the form of the March of the Living or similar educational trips, has caused much discussion, conflict and emotion in Melbourne and Sydney. In 1988 Holocaust survivors in Melbourne presented the Jewish Community Council of Victoria with a petition containing the signatures of over one thousand survivors who opposed the proposed participation in the commemorations in Poland by organized groups from Australia.[91] In 1989 the Jewish Community Council of Victoria, after listening for two hours to pleas from survivors and descendants against the concept of organized Jewish trips to Poland, voted to endorse the Executive Council of Australian Jewry (ECAJ) policy calling for a halt, for the time being, of all organized tours to Poland and calling on the ECAJ to forward these sentiments to the Israeli leadership.[92] Similarly, in Sydney, for many years the Australian Association of Jewish Holocaust Survivors and Descendants (AAJHS&D, before 1994 the AAJHS) recommended that community organizations not finance the programme. Holocaust survivor, Alex Weinberger opposed the trips, 'Poland is a graveyard, it is a cursed land ... The land has always been seen as an accessory'.[93] Survivors were not alone in their opposition to the tours; objections were raised from a range of sources, on a number of grounds. The development of a Holocaust tourist trade was a major concern. It was feared that hotels would be built next to the camps to accommodate tourists and that the camps would become part of a tourist's itinerary, with companies competing in offering the 'best deals'. According to Rabbi Raymond Apple of the Great Synagogue, 'These types of visits will trivialize the Holocaust ... it's better not to go back'.[94]

Alarm was voiced that Jewish tourism would result in good public relations for Poland and that this would take the focus away from Polish anti-Semitism during and after the Second World War and the current uneasy state of Polish–Jewish relations. Mendel Gelberman, Australian Institute of Holocaust Studies convener and Holocaust survivor, asserted: 'It [Poland] is still an antisemitic country and I don't believe they have changed their color ... If children wish to learn first-hand about the Holocaust, they should talk to survivors here'.[95] Moreover, it was argued that the trips would benefit the economy of an allegedly anti-Semitic Poland. Michael Gawenda wrote of a 'March of the Living circus':

> The idea of thousands of people marching on Auschwitz waving flags is a travesty of what a visit to a cemetery ought to be. A cemetery is not a place for pageants. A cemetery, especially a cemetery the size of Auschwitz's unfathomable horrors, is not a place that ought to be transformed into the site for political parade. That is what this march is a piece of political theatre, a piece of marketing driven triumphalism.[96]

In response to these concerns the United Israel Appeal consistently stressed that the programme was an 'experience' and part of an integrated educational programme, not mere 'sightseeing'.[97] Yoni Shapira, UIA Young Leadership Director and coordinator of the proposed Australian contingent, asserted:

> This will not be just a tour; the intention is for the participants to return to Australia as emissaries of change, with a commitment to putting something back into the community on the subjects of Holocaust awareness and Israel. It is imperative that future generations be made aware of the enormity of the Holocaust ... A venture such as this is the most effective means of education.[98]

Jewish youth tended to support the trips. Australasian Union of Jewish Students (AUJS) vice-president, Julia Cohen, said: 'the trips are essential ... the best way coming generations can get any understanding of what our relatives and fellow Jews experienced'.[99] Similarly, Mount Sinai College Jewish Studies director, Eileen Franklin, said about her recent participation in a WIZO trip to Poland, 'I didn't understand the size of the number – six million – until I saw the rooms of shoes and clothes. I realized that each piece of clothing belonged to a person and that person to a family and that family to a community.'[100] Not all Holocaust survivors were against MOTL. Dr Mark Spigelman, Treasurer of the AAJHS&D, pointed out that first-hand experience was necessary for young people:

> Events of the Holocaust are so bizarre and unbelievable that even today, with many of us survivors still alive, revisionism is taking hold ... What will happen when we, the ageing remnants, are no longer there to say 'but it did happen, I was there' and if our children and grandchildren are not there to say 'I have seen it, I was told about it'? I am going to Poland because I consider it my duty to make sure that those dedicated young men and women have first-hand knowledge of what happened.[101]

For over a decade Australian youth did not participate in MOTL, largely out of respect to the objections of survivors.[102] However, the meticulously prepared educational programme presented by Sue Hampel and Frances Prince, Mount Scopus College Jewish Studies coordinators and Holocaust educators who initiated the sending of an Australian delegation to join the 2001 MOTL, rendered many of the survivors' objections invalid. After being interviewed participants are prepared emotionally, educationally and spiritually through attendance at an extensive programme run over three months. Moreover, the Poland component of the trip focuses not only on death and destruction but also on the richness and diversity of Jewish life in Eastern Europe before the Holocaust. In addition, students meet with Polish teenagers to help break down negative stereotypes and build bridges. Most significantly, survivors are considered an integral part of the programme, sharing their personal stories both in the pre-departure educational activities and during the tour itself.

Many participants on the 2001 MOTL stressed how they had gained from the trip and how that knowledge would assist them in educating future generations about the Holocaust.[103] As a result, more Holocaust survivors became convinced of the positive impact of the tours.[104] In 2001, the Melbourne-based Descendants of the *Shoah* group voted in favour of the March and even donated $4,800 to the Victorian contingent.[105] However, just when it appeared that a consensus had been reached amongst Australian Jewry on the subject, another problem arose which was to cause further divisions in the community. In 2002 the New York-based March of the Living International, supported by many communities around the world, decided to cancel the Israel part of the programme due to security concerns stemming from a wave of suicide attacks. While some, who feared for the safety of their loved ones, accepted this decision, others vehemently opposed it. Sue Hampel stressed that the Israel component was essential, as part of the healing process and as a show of solidarity with Israel. Many argued that now more than any other time Diaspora Jewry should be demonstrating solidarity and support for with Israel.[106] As one prospective participant asked: 'What message would we be sending Israel if we were to say that it's safer to travel to Poland, where six million of our people were murdered, and not to Israel – the Jewish homeland'.[107] In the end the decision was taken away from the organizers when they were forced to abandon the second leg of the tour due to a dramatic surge in violence after which Federal Government advice warned Australians to 'defer all travel to Israel until further notice'.[108] For the time being, a consensus has been reached in regard to the nature of future tours to Poland. In 2003 MOTL international decided that participants will go to Poland and Israel, or neither.

There is no doubt that participants on MOTL, particularly during commemorating *Yom haShoah* in Poland and *Yom ha'Atzmaut* in Israel, experience a heightened feeling of belonging and unity with the Jewish people. Yet, as this case study of 'return visits' to Poland highlights, the very essence of the idea of 'returning to Poland' and its practice has also been highly contentious and a cause of tensions within Jewish communities.

Despite the high level of cohesion achieved by the collective mourning, Holocaust remembrance activities have also been occasions of conflict and disunity. Conflicts surrounding a variety of aspects of *Yom haShoah* commemorations, ranging from attendance to the performance of the religious rituals, has for most of the past fifty years been a continuing source of disappointment and frustration for organizers and Holocaust survivors in Australia, Britain and New Zealand who endeavoured and hoped for widespread Jewish presence and unity. Heated debates over the institution of a national Holocaust Memorial Day reflect an Anglo-Jewry unified in its engagement with the topic of how best to memorialize the Holocaust, although divided in its responses to it. The subject of organized tours to Poland led to tensions and antagonisms between various organizations in Australia and Britain. In Britain, this ill feeling has been further exacerbated by the suppression of some memories and perspectives in the interests of an appearance of consensus and unity.

Many have shared the aspiration for Jewish unity around Holocaust memorialization but the existence of differing approaches to the nature, form and content of Holocaust remembrance activities has meant that disunity within Jewish communities has sometimes been an unintended outcome. Holocaust memorialization has frequently been the occasion of intense debate and conflict about the appropriate institutional form that the collective act of remembering should take. This chapter suggests that a more intricate approach to the dynamics of the remembrance process is required; one that eschews broad generalizations about either unity or disunity, harmony or dispute.

6

A 'Universalist' Jewish Agenda?
An Australian Case Study

Do survivors of pain and trauma have a greater sensitivity and a heightened empathy towards the catastrophes and traumas of others, or does victimhood make one heartless towards those who have endured 'lesser tragedies'? Jews have suffered as a minority group throughout the ages. Has the pervasiveness of anti-Semitism and the centrality of the Holocaust in Jewish culture caused Jewish identification with human rights and social justice issues? Israeli historian and Holocaust survivor Saul Friedlander believes that Jews should be more tolerant than other people by virtue of their own experience. He has asserted that memory of the Holocaust 'imposes on us the duty of a moral vigilance keener than ever before, because of our awareness of the existence of a potential for "radical evil" within human society'.[1]

How have Holocaust survivors and their descendants interpreted, prioritized and acted on their understandings of the lessons and meanings of the Holocaust? Australian Jewry has been selected for this case study as it includes a high percentage of Holocaust survivors and descendants. This chapter questions whether the prominence of the Holocaust in Australian Jewish consciousness has led to increased Jewish concern with, and activism for, the needs of other and more disadvantaged minorities in Australia. Has the Holocaust been used as a pedagogic tool for encouraging universal humanistic values and moral behaviours, such as the defence of minority rights, the critical function of individual responsibility in a democratic society and the imperative to fight against prejudice, discrimination and racism? Has the recurrence of behaviours common during the Holocaust, such as stereotyping, scapegoating, prejudice, intolerance, blind obedience to a state that fosters unethical and immoral acts, and passivity in the face of evil, been condemned by Australian Jews?

First, it is important to set these questions about Australian Jewish understandings of the lessons and meanings of the Holocaust within the context of the nature of Australian Jewry. In his extensive study of the

Australian Jewish community, Professor Bill Rubinstein argues that:

> The post-war Jewish community was, and still more increasingly is, non-universalistic, deliberately rejecting any universal mission of the Jewish people to bring about a wider reform or radical agenda throughout the whole of society. Australian Jewry was non-universalistic in outlook in all or virtually all of its central institutions and representative bodies from at least the early–mid 1950s onwards … It is, rather, inward looking, concerned almost solely with its own future, with Jewish issues and an exclusively Jewish agenda.[2]

As we have seen in chapter three, Rubinstein's inward-looking designation of Australian Jewry is supported by my analysis of *Yom haShoah* (Holocaust Day) commemorations and representations of the Holocaust in museums. The former revealed a strong focus on the transmission of Jewish lessons of the Holocaust but a dearth of the universal humanistic ones.[3] Indeed, the unarticulated understanding that predominated was that universal solutions had failed to prevent the extermination of six million Jews. What was needed to prevent a reoccurrence was self-defence and self-reliance in the form of a sovereign Jewish state, vigilance against anti-Semitism and neo-Nazism, and world Jewish solidarity and mutual aid. Likewise, until the late 1990s, transmission of the universal humanistic lessons of the Holocaust was not a high priority in Holocaust museums.

Similar trends were found in Australian Jewish day schools where there has been no systematic or comprehensive coverage of the universal significance of the Holocaust.[4] The wider claims of multicultural Australia have been less significant for Holocaust education at Australian Jewish high schools than the imperative felt by committed Jews that Jewish youth must know, remember and perpetuate the memory of the Holocaust. Israeli novelist A.B. Yehoshua has pointed out that:

> our having been victims does not accord us any special moral standing. The victim does not become virtuous for having been a victim. Although the Holocaust inflicted a great injustice upon us, it does not grant us a certificate of everlasting righteousness. The murderers were amoral; the victims were not made moral.[5]

Educationalists in Australian Jewish high schools have, in the main, not heeded the warning that the universal lessons of the Holocaust must be conveyed to their students too.

These interpretations of the lessons of the Holocaust which have been conveyed at public forms of Holocaust remembrance have both reflected and further reinforced mainstream Australian Jewry's inward-looking orientation. Moreover, in contexts beyond formal Holocaust remembrance functions, Australian Jewish leaders rarely issued statements appealing to the moral conscience of Australian Jews to make connections between Jewish experiences of the Holocaust and the suffering of others in Australia or elsewhere.

Mainstream Australian Jewry has not prioritized the ethical tradition of *Tikkun Olam*, the commandment to Jews to heal, repair and transform the world. Australian Jewry's overwhelmingly inward-looking orientation for most of the past fifty years is explained not only by the precedence given to Jewish survival after the Holocaust, but also by a number of additional, interrelated factors. Firstly, for the first three decades after the Holocaust the Jewish community on the whole conformed to the monoculturalism of Australian society and politics that determined the widespread non-involvement of immigrant groups in Australian politics.[6] Mainstream Jewish organizations would not have felt comfortable involving themselves with movements critical of Australian society as in doing so they may have appeared ungrateful for Australia's acceptance of Jewish refugees from Nazism. A second factor restricting Australian Jewry's political involvement to issues relating to the Jewish community and to Israel was that more Jews were becoming middle class. Jewish socio-economic interests had moved them away from the social agendas of the Left. Thirdly, the anti-Zionism of the far left, worldwide and in Australia, which emerged in the wake of Israel's 1967 Six Day War, served to strengthen the trend of Australian Jewry (and North American Jewry) towards non-universalism and neo-conservatism, and further marginalized the small Jewish left groups, such as the Australian Jewish Democratic Society (AJDS), which remained.[7]

However, from the mid-to-late-1990s a significant change has been occurring in the nature of Australian Jewry. A number of commentators have pointed to increased interest and concern of mainstream Jewish organizations with broader Australian cultural, social and political contexts. Sam Lipski, former editor of the *Australian Jewish News* (*AJN*), has asserted that 'only in the 90s have the bulk of communally involved Australian Jews, and much of their leadership, moved to a more "American style" concern for the wider issues'.[8] Likewise, Melbourne academic Philip Mendes has identified over the past ten years 'Jewish involvement in newer single-issue radical movements based principally on the politics of identity, rather than class'.[9] This chapter presents evidence of recent Jewish involvement with anti-racist education, Aboriginal rights, and with issues relating to refugees and asylum seekers, particularly to their internment in Detention Centres.

A number of interrelated factors have contributed to this changing orientation of Australian Jewry. Certainly immigrant and ethnic group participation in politics has been facilitated by Australian multi-culturalism. Generational factors are also at play. Post-war Australian-born Jews feel secure and at home in their country of birth. In contrast to many of their parents who came as refugees, they have come of age in an environment where Jewish survival is no longer a threat. This feeling of security enables them to feel free to join social movements that are critical of Australian society and politics without worrying about accusations of ingratitude. Jewish communal politics has played a part too, including the re-affiliation of the AJDS to the Jewish Community Council of Victoria (JCCV) and the Left liberal-leaning editorship of the *AJN* for much of the past decade which has produced a politically pluralistic Jewish weekly.[10] Also, as Philip Mendes has pointed out, this recent Australian Jewish universalist trend 'seems to be a carbon copy of traditional American Jewish universalism, and perhaps reflects the influence of globalization and the internet over the ten years with increasing connections between the two communities'.[11]

Yet these developments alone do not explain increased Australian Jewish participation in public debates in Australia. It is my contention that a significant source of this more outward-looking orientation has come from Holocaust survivors and their descendants who have, increasingly over the past five years or so, been applying their actual or vicarious memories of the Holocaust to Australian social and political contexts.[12] Their interpretations of the Holocaust and its meanings include not only Jewish, but also universal humanistic lessons. These understandings are in turn impacting on the wider Jewish community, bringing about broader Australian Jewish engagement with human rights and social justice issues in Australia. Before turning our attention to some of those issues, it is first necessary to explain the timing of this changed orientation. Why is it that Holocaust survivors and their descendants are having this particular impact on the nature of Australian Jewry at the turn of the millennium, and not at any stage earlier?

A number of interrelated factors, many connected to the stage of survivors and their descendants in the life cycle, but also to do with the elevated status of survivors (and indeed of victimhood) worldwide, account for the timing of this development. The increased centrality of the Holocaust in world Jewish culture from the late 1970s led to an interest in the stories of those who had survived. This attention to the testimony of survivors coincided with the end of their working years. Upon retirement many Holocaust survivors had time to reflect on their lives. Contemplation of their Holocaust experiences led some to respond sensitively and compassionately to the traumas of other persecuted people. The children of Holocaust survivors, the 'Second Generation' of Holocaust survivors, are now adults in mid-life with more time on their hands to reflect on their parents' trauma. Over the past decade the consciousness and profile of the Second Generation has been raised as they have become involved in the activities of the Sydney and Melbourne Holocaust museums, have established Second Generation groups, and have contributed to edited publications about their experiences of growing up in the shadow of the Holocaust.[13] While some of the sons and daughters of survivors have become involved in Jewish community organizations and affairs, others have looked outwards, and have spoken with moral voices and taken moral actions on issues beyond the traditional Jewish communal agenda. Their parents' experiences under Nazism inspired some to work towards making the world a better place, not just for Jews, but also for oppressed people anywhere. Many of the grandchildren of Holocaust survivors, those of the 'Third Generation' of Holocaust survivors, have acquired formal knowledge about the Holocaust from their education at Australian Jewish high schools and are applying that knowledge to social and political issues in Australian society. One of those issues has been racism.

Has the Jewish experience of centuries of anti-Semitism and racism, culminating in the Holocaust, led to Australian Jewish engagement with issues of racism in Australia? Jews and indigenous Australians have a common heritage of suffering and displacement as victims of racism. Has this led to a special Jewish awareness and sensitivity to the torments of indigenous Australians?

During the mid-to-late-1990s, mainstream Australian Jewry became involved in the struggle against racism, in particular against the policies of Pauline Hanson and the One Nation party. Many Jewish community organizations have been disappointed by Prime Minister John Howard's failure to repudiate Hanson's racist statements and her attacks on multiculturalism, Asian immigrants and Australian Aboriginals. The Australia–Israel and Jewish Affairs Council (AIJAC), the Executive Council of Australian Jewry (ECAJ), the Orthodox rabbinate, the Australian Council of Christians and Jews, the *AJN*, the National Conference of Jewish Women, Melbourne's Temple Beth Israel, as well as many community leaders all called for a tougher response from the

Prime Minister.[14] However, the question to be asked is whether the Jewish community has been vigorous and determined *enough* in its opposition to racism in Australia?

Jewish responses to racism were not limited to rhetoric but included a significant contribution to anti-racist education. Various groups have held public meetings within the community about the Hansonite threat. As part of 1997 anti-racism week, Melbourne's *B'nai B'rith* Anti-Defamation Commission (BB ADC) and the Jewish Community Council of Victoria (JCCV) held a seminar to 'reflect, assess, and develop a communal approach to Australia's Race Debate and the Jewish community'. Themes covered included national reconciliation and Jewish Aboriginal relations, race politics, and moral responsibility after the Holocaust. Executive director of the BB ADC, Danny Ben-Moshe, insisted that the anti-racist message needed to be conveyed to the Jewish community too, urging Jewish day schools to educate about racism in Australian society.[15] Ben-Moshe would have been pleasantly surprised when in 1998 Jewish students, under a banner 'The Jewish Community Says No to Racism', joined a student demonstration against One Nation in Melbourne.[16] Two Jewish high school students addressed the gathering, both drawing parallels with pre-war Germany. Year 10 student David Sztrajt said:

> As a Jew, I know the effects of racial hatred and intolerance ... I like most of the Jewish people, lost family members in the Holocaust when Adolf Hitler came to power in Germany and spread his anti-Semitic views. The world stood in silence as anti-Semitism spread and the Jewish people paid the ultimate price ... Now in Australia in 1998, we are clearly faced with racism in politics ... As racist views seep through our society, we can't afford to stand in silence. Because we didn't stand on the flame when it was only a spark, it is now time to stand together as a proud multicultural Australia and put out the fire.[17]

Experiences of the Holocaust, actual and vicarious, have led some Jews to become actively involved in the struggle against racism. Over the past five years, the aims of Holocaust museums in Australia, run predominantly by Holocaust survivors and their descendants, have evolved to include not only education about the events that overcame European Jewry between 1933 and 1945 and its Jewish lessons, but transmission of universal humanistic lessons of the Holocaust too. According to the President of the Jewish Holocaust Museum and Research Centre in Melbourne, the task of the museum was not only to show the horrors of the Holocaust but also to show what racism, prejudice, intolerance and the lack of understanding can lead to.[18] Many of the survivors who work at the museum have come to believe that it is vital to protect the rights of vulnerable and disadvantaged groups. The President of Melbourne's Child Survivors Group explained:

> The volunteers of the Holocaust Museum have undertaken a huge and ambitious task: to teach the young the importance of tolerance, respect and acceptance of those with different beliefs. Every week the hundreds of school students who visit the Centre experience a revelation they will not forget. Many understand the importance of not becoming indifferent bystanders.[19]

The Jewish Holocaust Museum and Research Centre's activities have evolved and broadened according to its aims. The museum's programme for the Jewish and wider community was initially limited to educational sessions on specific aspects on the Holocaust and seminars for Victorian school teachers on 'Teaching the Holocaust'. In July 2000 the museum organized a day seminar on racism for school teachers from all over Melbourne. The keynote speech was entitled 'Racism in schools, Myth or Reality?' and a panel discussion on the question included indigenous and ethnic speakers who provided Aboriginal and multicultural perspectives on racism.[20] The museum's staff are not only concerned with racism when it is anti-Semitism, rather, their sensitivity to anti-Semitism has extended to racism directed at others.

The Sydney Jewish Museum is equally committed to educating against racism. One Holocaust survivor who volunteers at the museum stated:

> I see it as a mission to tell the children – our future – the truth about racism and hatred of people who are 'different'. It has never been more important to spread this message than today, when we are seeing Holocaust deniers trying to make race hatred acceptable and the rise, again, of racist political parties all over the world.[21]

Another Jewish community initiative to create a more tolerant Australian society has been the 'Courage to Care' exhibition.[22] The exhibition, whose basis is the stories of rescued and rescuers rather than a narrative of the Holocaust itself, aims to convey a message of the importance of living in harmony with others, and the need to stand up against racism, discrimination and prejudice, particularly in relation to minority groups. The exhibition is supplemented by a special educational programme on tolerance, 'Living in Harmony', in which experienced facilitators run workshops encouraging student discussion on contemporary issues of discrimination, racism and anti-Semitism. In this way the students are provided with an opportunity to relate the material and message of the exhibition to real-life situations, such as bullying in the school-ground, multiculturalism and racism, and aboriginality. One of the Holocaust survivors who tours with the museum said, 'It is an exhibition about educating the children about tolerance. And to show them that if there is one individual that stands up, it makes a difference.'[23]

There are also indications that the traditionally parochial orientation of Holocaust commemorations, focusing almost exclusively on the Jewish lessons of the Holocaust, are gradually changing. Expressions of a more outward-looking understanding of the Holocaust and its significance have begun to emerge, especially since survivors have given testimony from the early 1990s and the younger generation, usually grandchildren of Holocaust survivors, gained a voice through the institution of a 'youth address'. At the 1996 Holocaust commemorations in Perth, both the MC and the youth speaker not only condemned the passivity of the world during the Holocaust but also since, during the Cambodian, Rwandan and Bosnian crises. They stressed the obligation of Jews to be at the forefront of the struggle against genocide anywhere in the world.[24] At a commemoration in Melbourne in 2000 the national president of the Australian Union of Jewish Students (AUJS) stated that Holocaust commemorations served not only to perpetuate the memories of those who survived but also to warn against the dangers of apathy and indifference.[25]

Australian Jewish responses to the racist threat have not been limited to educational efforts to alleviate racism in the present but also have included demands for an acknowledgement of, and apology for, past wrongdoings committed against Australia's indigenous peoples. Many Jews have perceived commonalities between denial of the Stolen Generations and Holocaust denial.[26] Senator Aden Ridgeway's comparisons between denial of the Stolen Generations expressed by the Aboriginal Affairs minister (John Heron) and Holocaust denial were supported by Alan Gold who insisted:

> Who better to understand the disgust of the Aborigines with our politicians than we Jews? ... And shouldn't we Jews be taking the lead in helping the Aborigines defend themselves against the onslaught of this government?[27]

Ron Castan, one of Australia's most prominent QCs and the lead counsel in the Mabo Land Rights case, asserted that 'The refusal to apologise for dispossession, for massacres, and for the theft of children, is the Australian equivalent of the Holocaust deniers – those who say it never really happened'.[28] He asserted that all Australians must fully acknowledge the most shameful episode in Australian history, suggesting that Jews lead the drive to establish a museum of the Stolen and the Dispossessed, and erect memorials of remembrance, 'sorry monuments', at sites of Aboriginal massacres.[29]

Jewish academics and scholars have been particularly outspoken in support of Aboriginal rights. Amongst those criticizing John Howard's attitude towards Aboriginal reconciliation and restitution and his persistent refusal to apologize formally for past wrongs to indigenous Australians, have been Robert Manne, Professor of Politics at La Trobe University, Colin Tatz, Director of the Australian Institute of Holocaust and Genocide Studies and Jewish writers at the Sydney Writers festival.[30] Both Geoffrey Levey, lecturer in Jewish Studies at Sydney University, and retired Jewish History professor Bernard Rechter challenged the award of an honorary doctorate to Prime Minister John Howard by Bar Ilan University in Israel. Both were disturbed by the decision in the light of John Howard's non-humanitarian record. Rechter asked provocatively, 'Would Bar-Ilan have honoured him had the stolen children been Jewish or the refugees been DP's refusing to return to the graveyards of Poland and Germany?'[31] Aboriginal rights were not just the concern of individual Jewish scholars and intellectuals but were on the communal agenda too. The ECAJ urged Federal Government to endorse the recommendations of the Stolen Children Enquiry.[32] A wide cross section of Jewish communal leaders supported this call and there was significant Jewish attendance at Melbourne and Sydney's 'Walk for Reconciliation' 2000, which demanded an apology to the Stolen Generations.[33]

As with Jewish involvement in the struggle against racism, the motivation to fight for indigenous causes was frequently explained as emanating from a consciousness of the persecution and displacement of the Jewish people throughout history.[34] The President of the Australian Jewish Historical Society declared: 'We, as members of the Jewish community of this country, have a special responsibility to understand what has happened ... There are such forceful similarities to our own collective experiences, that for us this [Stolen Generations] report is personal.'[35]

Australian Jewish involvement in the struggle for Aboriginal rights and the fight against racism are both expressions of a more universalistic

Australian Jewry.[36] Yet both were easy and non-threatening causes that led to very little communal conflict. Likewise, issues relating to refugees in the 1990s were not particularly divisive. The Australian Jewish community was active in raising funds for refugees from Rwanda, Bosnia, Kosovo and East Timor. In 1994 a group of Melbourne Jews, many of them children of Holocaust survivors, responded to the Rwandan tragedy by establishing Keshet, the Australian Jewish human-itarian relief appeal. A Keshet flier read 'Help Keshet let the world know that the Jews of Australia understand about the repression of a people, the plight of the displaced person and their need for help.'[37] Jewish schools in Melbourne and Sydney became involved in the fundraising project through activities such as uniform-free days.[38] A Yiddish Benefit Concert was organized through the Kadimah, the communal and cultural centre for Melbourne's Yiddish-speaking community. As child of Holocaust survivors and author Arnold Zable explained, it was the place of the Holocaust in Australian Jewish consciousness which led to these efforts.

> One of the lessons that emerges from the Shoah, which was our darkest hour, is while it's important to find refuge for Jews, it's also important to try and help others who are facing a similar plight. We must maintain sympathy and understanding … Looking after one's own as well as looking after others must go hand in hand. We must always be aware of what's happening to other people. There are now 21 million refugees in the world. Unfortunately, it is an ongoing problem.[39]

The ECAJ made a very public condemnation of the atrocities perpetrated in Bosnia in the mid-1990s, joined forces with the Australian Federation of Islamic Councils to call on Australia to make strong representations to the UN, and appealed to the Jewish community to give generously to relief campaigns. A letter from a group of Jewish high school students urged the Jewish community to do something to help the Bosnian Muslims. 'As grandchildren of Holocaust survivors, we are horrified to see a second Holocaust in the making … We as Jews have a responsibility to our fellow-nations to prevent a Holocaust happening again.'[40]

As with the Rwandan and Bosnian tragedies, scenes from Kosovo in 1999 also evoked images of the Holocaust. One Holocaust survivor declared:

As a survivor of the Holocaust who has been in similar situations I know and understand too well the Kosovars' traumas ... How well I know the feeling of being dispossessed, of having to leave home and of being separated from my family. And now, during my lifetime I see it happening again albeit to people of another minority and religion.[41]

Jewish youth movements, AUJS and schools in Melbourne united in efforts to fundraise, selling coloured ribbons for $2 to raise awareness to help the homeless and hungry refugees from Kosovo. 'We decided we should not be the generation who sat back and watched silently; instead we had to take action',[42] stated the organizers. Community leaders welcomed the government's decision to offer temporary asylum to four thousand Kosovar Albanians but said that it was not enough and called for an increase in Australia's humanitarian migrant intake. Later, the government's decision not to allow the Kosovars to remain permanently was criticized.[43] Suzanne Rutland deplored the government's lack of generosity and fear mongering, declaring that:

> We as a Jewish community must speak out ... We must remind the Australian public that countries which take in refugees stand to benefit at all levels. Having experienced dislocation and trauma, refugees work hard to contribute to their country of adoption because in their hour of need, they were offered a refuge. So, let us be more generous in allowing those who are suffering from persecution and trauma the chance to learn to smile again in our lucky country.[44]

The 1999 East Timor crisis also drew Jewish opinion and action. A range of organizations were involved in an array of activities, including rallies, fundraising, protests, demonstrations, demands and lobbying.[45] Letters were written to the Federal Government expressing Jewish community concern; the plight of the East Timorese was the subject of sermons, prayers and appeals at several synagogues during *Yom Kippur*, Steven Kolt initiated and led a 'stay away from Bali and Indonesia' campaign; Keshet raised over $20,000 for East Timor;[46] *B'nai B'rith* District 21 donated medical supplies;[47] calls were made for the instigation of a UN war crimes tribunal to bring the perpetrators of crimes in East Timor to account;[48] the AJDS organized a petition to Keating, and a Holocaust survivor called on fellow survivors and their descendants to march in solidarity with the East Timorese under a 'Concentration Camp

Survivors in solidarity with East Timor' banner. A group of academics who teach Holocaust and Genocide Studies wrote to Foreign Minister Alexander Downer, drawing analogies with the Holocaust and urging Australians not to stand by as signs of a full genocide emerged: 'We must act, and not simply speak'.[49]

The *Tampa* crisis in September 2001, during which a boatload of 460 asylum seekers were rescued at sea by the Norwegian freighter *MV Tampa* but drifted helplessly, having been refused refuge in Australia, evoked memories of the Holocaust and drew Australian Jewish condemnation of the government's response as lacking in human-itarianism.[50] Parallels were drawn between the *Tampa* and boatloads of Jewish refugees that were refused sanctuary (the *Exodus, Struma, Patria* and the *SS Louis*). Letters to the *AJN* recalled the plight of the *St Louis* which in 1939, carrying German Jewish refugees, was refused permission to land in Cuba, the US and elsewhere and was forced to return to Europe, where most perished in the Holocaust. Victims of Nazi oppression and their offspring were urged to make their stand known.[51] Sam Lipski, child of pre-war refugees from Nazism, declared:

> when it comes to refugees, the Australian Jewish community has the motivation, experience, human and material resources, and the political access to the major political parties to try to make a differ-ence. We must make use of these advantages because we owe it to Australia and ourselves never again to watch and stand idly by.[52]

It was stressed that people on the *Tampa* had reached that same stage of utter desperation that those on board the *St Louis* had experienced.[53] Former Melbourne University historian, and child of Holocaust survivors, Mark Baker, protested to John Howard when he visited the Australia–Israel Chamber of Commerce. The placard he held read 'St Louis, 1939. Exodus, 1947. Tampa, 2001'.[54] One of Baker's supporters accused those attending the meeting of being too concerned about the political and business implications of criticizing the Howard government:

> we as Jews have an obligation to take the humanitarian path regard-less of the political implications. It is time for our leading Jewish citizens to think seriously about our heritage and to give all people, particularly those escaping oppressive regimes, 'a fair go'.[55]

Australian Jewish approaches to issues of refugees and asylum seekers became considerably more complex following the September 11 suicide bombings in the US by Muslim *al-Qaeda* terrorists, the ensuing war on terror in Afghanistan, and the ferocious second Palestinian *intifada* against Israel in which waves of suicide bombers have claimed hundreds of lives, terrorizing and traumatizing Israeli society and Jews worldwide. Most of the recent asylum seekers to Australia, including those on the Tampa, have been Muslims from Afghanistan. There have also been significant numbers of Iraqi, Palestinian and other asylum-seekers from the Middle East. Jewish responses to Muslim and Middle Eastern asylum seekers in Australia must be understood in the context of their concern for Israel's survival and the atmosphere of increased anti-Semitism threatening the security of Jews worldwide. These circumstances have meant that there has been a clash between humanitarian values on the one hand, and Australian Jewish fears about the expected anti-Semitism of the latest arrivals on the other. As a result, there is no clear consensus, no 'Australian Jewish position', on this particular wave of asylum seekers. Through the second half of 2001 and the first half of 2002, debate about asylum seekers was widespread through the pages of the *AJN*. The many letters on the subject reflected the breadth and depth of opinion.

The internment and treatment of refugees and asylum seekers in detention centres such as Woomera, Curtin, Port Hedland and Maribyrnong instigated passionate Australian Jewish responses. Jewish groups and individuals appealed for a more humane approach to their processing. Some not only criticized the government's prolonged and inhumane detention of asylum seekers in oppressive conditions, but also suggested an increase to Australia's refugee intake; others recommended that all asylum seekers should be released except those considered a threat due to criminal or terrorist background and pleaded with the government to screen asylum seekers more quickly.[56] The ECAJ passed a resolution calling on the Federal Government to ensure fair and humanitarian treatment of refugees and a review of mandatory detention of asylum seekers.[57]

Australian Jewish support for asylum seekers was not restricted to words. Dana Krause, a Jewish paralegal working in immigration law, is a regular visitor at the Maribyrnong Detention Centre. She reported to the *AJN* about the effects of detention on the children in Woomera where she spent three days. Her inspiration for working with refugees came from stories of her grandmother's persecution and survival in the Holocaust. 'I guess it's the helplessness I felt about the Holocaust translated into helping other people.'[58] Arnold Zable writes of the close affinity he has with the asylum seekers at Maribyrnong Detention Centre where he is a regular visitor too. As part of his efforts to gain support for ending mandatory detention for asylum seekers he conveyed his eye-witness testimony of children and adults suffering from trauma, severe depression and extreme distress.[39] Zable explained that his compassion comes from close to his heart. 'Inside Maribyrnong Detention Centre I have heard many variations of my mother's story ... I'm alive today because my mother was a queue jumper ... Jews should know there are certain times when there are no queues and you have to run for your life'.[60]

Members of the Child Survivors of the Holocaust group are among a number of Jewish organizations visiting asylum seekers regularly at Maribyrnong Detention Centre. A founder of the group, Dr Paul Valent, has been critical of the Federal Government's immigration policy and has lobbied to have the detention centres closed. Valent, who sees his own family history reflected in the stories of asylum seekers who flee persecution, believes that Jews are still unwilling to stand up and voice their experiences of trauma for fear of drawing attention to themselves but, he asserts, 'If the Jewish community believes that most of the nations during WWII [*sic*] were too silent and did nothing well then they should do something themselves now'.[61]

A Jewish vigil at Maribyrnong Detention Centre in March 2002 attracted over five hundred Jews. The vigil was organized by Jews for Refugees, a humanitarian organization, and supported by diverse Jewish community groups, including Orthodox and Progressive Rabbis. The participants protested against Australia's treatment of refugees, brought them *matzah* (unleavened bread), sung Pesach (Passover) songs and demanded their freedom.[62] Jewish youth, out in force, were organised by 'Jewish Youth for Refugees'.[63] In her speech, Dalit Kaplan, granddaughter to four Holocaust survivors, expressed the group's objection to the inhumane treatment of asylum seekers in detention centres and asserted her understanding that 'the passive bystanders are the reason why the Holocaust happened. People have got a humanitarian responsibility to involve themselves in such an issue ... As Jews we empathise with their plight and feel a strong moral responsibility to assist the asylum seekers.'[64] Later in 2002, Jews for Refugees, together with two Muslims on temporary protection visas and a detention centre guard, built a *succah*, a shelter that is a symbol of Jewish asylum, at Maribyrnong. David Zyngier, child of Holocaust survivors and publicity officer of Jews for Refugees said: 'As Jews we treasure our Jewish tradition. We wanted to contemporise our Jewish traditions and give them meaning to what is going on in Australia today'.[65]

While some Australian Jews gave the asylum seekers their unreserved assistance, many others offered their support conditionally.

Some Middle-Eastern asylum seekers show no empathy, tolerance or understanding towards Jews. In fact, some have displayed loathing, as in the celebrations post-September 11 in northern Melbourne and western Sydney by some new arrivals and relatives already residing here, and the endorsement by some detainees at Port Hedland of acts of terrorism in Israel. Anyone who is escaping from tyranny should be given a safe haven – provided they leave their prejudicial baggage on shore at the time of arrival.[66]

Many Australian Jews felt that these conditions had not been reached. There were complaints about the behaviour of the current asylum seekers, including their use of violence, destruction of documents and alleged exploitation of children for political purposes.[67] Erwin Lamm, who came out to Australia on the *Dunera* in 1940 and was interned for two years upon arrival from Britain, compared the behaviour of the *Dunera* boys and present day asylum seekers. 'We certainly didn't burn anything down. We never went on a hunger strike … we waited our turn.'[68] It was commonly believed by Australian Jews, as by wider Australian society, that the refugees should cooperate with the authorities and be grateful that they are away from the repressive regimes from which they had fled, even if it meant being in detention centres.[69]

Some contributors to the debate perceived Jewish support for Muslim and Middle Eastern asylum seekers and the security of Israel and of Jews worldwide as mutually exclusive causes. They held that only a united Jewish front could tackle the threats of rising anti-Zionism and anti-Semitism. It was argued that large-scale admission of fundamentalist Muslims, who it was alleged, would not accept Australia's pluralistic society, threatened Jewish life in Australia. Bill Rubinstein drew on statistics to demonstrate the dangers presented by the rapid increase in the Muslim population relative to the Australian Jewish community. Rubinstein pointed out that within a few decades there may be half-a-million Muslims in Australia, cautioning that such a voting lobby would not be ignored by governments.[70] The irate author of one letter to the *AJN* wrote:

These same people may end up firebombing your synagogue or attacking your wife or children … It's nice to be politically correct, but if only the local Muslims would show the same respect to Jews then I could be more understanding of their plight.[71]

These perspectives did not pass without criticism. A letter of warning asserted that the Jewish experience of being victims of stereotyping must lead them to distinguish between terrorists and other Muslims. 'As Jews we know how dangerous it is to stereotype an entire group of people based on the behaviour of a few.'[72] One of the founders of Jews for Refugees, insisted that 'If you are a supporter of Israel you have to be a supporter of refugees because Israel is a country of refugees who have fled persecution'.[73] Those rejecting the claim that Jewish universalism and survivalism could not coexist argued that inhumanity transcended religion and race. They insisted on the necessity to address the neglect of human beings.[74]

Without doubt the whole question of Australian Jewish support for asylum seekers has been complicated by the recent world events, specifically by the anti-Zionist and anti-Semitic propaganda spread by some Middle Eastern countries under the influence of militant Islam. JCCV President Grahame Leonard explained the quandary well.

> A lot of Australian Jews are faced with what they see as a terrible dilemma. On the one hand, they support refugees regardless of any creed or colour. On the other hand, they understand some are enemies of the Jews.[75]

Indeed, some Jews refrained from participating in the 2002 Palm Sunday rallies calling for compassion for refugees, not because of a lack of Jewish sympathy for such a cause but because of the involvement of groups campaigning against Israel. Many community bodies and individuals did not want to be associated with rallies that promoted anti-Israel propaganda.[76]

This chapter has demonstrated that Australian Jews have been increasingly involved in wider Australian social and political contexts, particularly with anti-racist education, Aboriginal rights and with issues relating to refugees and asylum seekers. I have argued that this is partly because some 'First', 'Second' and 'Third' generation Holocaust survivors are speaking publicly about their understandings of the Holocaust and its meanings. This is gradually producing a more widespread Australian Jewish recognition of the universal, as well as the Jewish lessons of the Holocaust, leading in turn to a more outward-looking Australian Jewry.[77]

These findings are only tentative at present. I am continuing my work in this area, aiming to establish the ways in which Holocaust survivors and their descendants have interpreted, prioritized and acted on their understandings of the lessons and meanings of the Holocaust. In addition, systematic research must be undertaken to ascertain to what extent Australian Jewry's outward-looking trend has extended beyond some intellectuals, community leaders and Holocaust survivors and their descendants, as identified in this chapter, to the grassroots community level. Another question concerns the relationship between Jewish participation in universalistic movements and Jewish particularistic concerns about the existence and potential revival of anti-Semitism in Australia. Have lived or vicarious experiences of the Holocaust led to genuine universalist outlooks or have some of those involved in outward-looking issues and causes been motivated by the assumption that a less racist society, and a greater tolerance of differences, will decrease anti-Semitism and make the world a safer place for Jews? Are these approaches mutually exclusive? In short, is Jewish involvement in universal humanistic cause an expression of altruism, pragmatic self-interest, or unconscious self-interest?

Very little research has been undertaken with regard to Holocaust survivors' understandings of the lessons of the Holocaust. As far as I am aware, no such research has been undertaken in Britain or New Zealand. Gillian Walnes of the Anne Frank Educational Trust UK touched on the topic when she asserted that 'Holocaust survivors are the ones who are determined not to just focus on the crimes of the past, but those of the present which affect people of all races, religions and creeds'.[78] Only further research can ascertain whether this statement indicates a further similarity in the ways in which the Holocaust has been remembered and understood in the Jewish Diaspora.

7

Afterword: The Past, Present and Future of Holocaust Memorialization

It has recently been argued by Bill Rubinstein that the evolution of Jewish communities in English-speaking countries has been broadly similar, despite the considerably different national histories of the countries where Jews resided.[1] Rubinstein's general argument is supported by this research. There are striking similarities in the ways in which the Holocaust has been memorialized in Australia, Britain and New Zealand, notwithstanding differences in the political, social and cultural histories in those countries, or the size of their Jewish populations and Holocaust survivor components.

Representations of the Holocaust and its meanings at *Yom haShoah* commemorations stress the uniquely Jewish aspects of the Holocaust. Rituals, cultural programmes and speeches have focused almost exclusively on the Jewish heroes, victims and survivors of the Holocaust. An outcome of this narrow focus is a correspondingly narrow consideration of the lessons of the Holocaust that have tended to focus on the Jewish lessons to the exclusion of consideration of the universal humanistic ones. Likewise, Holocaust museums and exhibitions in Australia, Britain and New Zealand have defined the event as the systematic annihilation of European Jewry, unequivocally asserting the uniqueness of Jewish suffering and fate. Yet by universalizing the Holocaust too, museums and exhibitions make themselves relevant for the multicultural, Western-orientated societies in whose midst they were established. Additional parallels in Holocaust remembrance patterns are found in the ways in which Holocaust memorialization has, at times, both unified and divided Jewish communities; as well as how the imagery and terminology of the Holocaust have been misused and misappropriated in Australia, Britain and New Zealand, for a variety of agendas. In contrast, the ways in which the Holocaust entered the mainstream cultures of each society presents one significant difference. Whereas Holocaust survivors were the main driving force in Australia and New Zealand, interested gentile individuals and groups in multicultural British society, guided by Jewish leadership elites, instigated and implemented Holocaust remembrance projects.

Yet there are signs that in the future Holocaust memorialization in these countries may increasingly diverge. Fifty years after the destruction of European Jewry, the generation of survivors of the Holocaust is slowly disappearing. How will the Holocaust be remembered after the demise of the surviving remnant? Will Holocaust memory be assimilated and absorbed by the dominant cultures in Australia, Britain and New Zealand? What is the future of Holocaust remembrance in an age of mass killings and genocides? Will the Holocaust be remembered as one of many tragedies of the twentieth and twenty-first centuries?

In Australia, not only the 'Second Generation', the children of Holocaust survivors, but also the 'Third Generation', many of whom have acquired formal knowledge about the Holocaust from their education at Australian Jewish day schools, have demonstrated their commitment to perpetuating memory of the Holocaust. The grandchildren of Holocaust survivors have been attending the main community *Yom haShoah* commemorations in increasing numbers, organizing Holocaust Awareness Week activities on university campuses, becoming involved in the activities of Holocaust museums, and arranging Holocaust seminars for Jewish youth. Kitia Altman, a Polish Holocaust survivor, recognized these encouraging signs for the perpetuation of social memory of the Holocaust in Australia after she addressed observances organized by Jewish students at Chisholm Institute and Melbourne University in 1990.

> We need not worry about who will take over the legacy of our horrific memories. We will leave them in the hearts of our youth. Our past will not be forgotten, the generation of our grandchildren will remember it while striving for a better future for mankind [*sic*].[2]

The signs are that Holocaust memorialization in New Zealand may dwindle after the passing of the survivors as their descendants are few and neither the Jewish nor broader communities have shown signs of taking responsibility for initiating and implementing Holocaust remembrance projects. The Second Generation in Britain are demographically stronger than their New Zealand counterparts but are still struggling with their own emotional issues and most have shown little inclination to take over the legacy of Holocaust memorialization.[3] In ethnically diverse Britain, where the Holocaust is utilized for anti-racist education, it remains to be seen whether the uniqueness of the Holocaust will continue to be stressed after the demise of survivors. It is conceivable that in the future, the destruction of European Jewry by the Nazis may be memorialized alongside a variety of massacres and genocides.

Indeed, other ethnic and indigenous groups also carry traumatic memories of past sufferings. This research project not only advances the knowledge base of Holocaust remembrance studies but also relates to a broader experience by raising the question of how traumatic collective memory is memorialized in modern societies. It is hoped that this book will provide a foundation for a future study of how the collective memories of past suffering of other ethnic or indigenous groups have impacted on their identity and self-representation to society at large. How has trauma been memorialized? Have some groups chosen to remember and preserve their memories for future generations, while others have preferred to forget? Have the dominant cultures represented their suffering and if so, in what ways? How have former victims of trauma related towards those currently suffering trauma and dislocation? These issues are clearly central to debates concerning asylum seekers, refugees, migrants and indigenous people in contemporary multicultural and culturally pluralistic societies.

Notes

CHAPTER 1

1. Michael Berenbaum, 'Who Owns the Holocaust?', *Centre News*, 20, 1 (April 2001), p.18.
2. Bill Rubinstein, personal communication, April 2003.
3. Rochelle Saidel, *Never Too Late To Remember* (London: Holmes & Meier, 1996); Michael Berenbaum, *After Tragedy and Triumph: Essays on Modern Jewish Thought and the American Experience* (Cambridge: Cambridge University Press, 1991).
4. James E. Young, *The Texture of Memory: Holocaust Memorials and Meaning* (New Haven, CT: Yale University Press, 1993).
5. Edward T. Linenthal, *Preserving Memory: The Struggle to Create America's Holocaust Museum* (New York: Penguin, 1995).
6. Yael Zerubavel, 'The Death of Memory and the Memory of Death: Masada and the Holocaust as Historical Metaphors', *Representations*, 45 (Winter 1994), pp.72–100; Yael Zerubavel, *Recovered Roots: Collective Memory and the Making of Israeli National Tradition* (London and Chicago: University of Chicago Press, 1995). For example, Zerubavel illustrates how feelings of Israeli vulnerability in the 1973 *Yom Kippur* War evoked greater identification with the victims of the Holocaust. Jews were no longer condemned for 'going like sheep to the slaughter', and the concept of heroism was broadened to include spiritual as well as physical resistance. Young, *Texture of Memory*.
7. Rabbi Irving Greenberg, *The Jewish Way: Living the Holidays* (New York: Touchstone, 1988), pp.314–72. See also Don Handelman and E. Katz, 'State Ceremonies of Israel – Remembrance Day and Independence Day', in Don Handelman (ed.), *Models and Mirrors: Towards an Anthropology of Public Events* (New York: Cambridge University Press, 1990).
8. One focus of Berenbaum's research was the debates surrounding the decision in 1979 to complement distinctly Jewish communal observance of *Yom haShoah* in the USA with State-sponsored 'National Days of Remembrance'; Michael Berenbaum, *After Tragedy*; Michael Berenbaum, 'On the Politics of Public Commemoration of the Holocaust', *Shoah* (Fall/Winter 1981–82), pp.6–9, 37; Michael Berenbaum, 'The Uniqueness and Universality of the Holocaust', *American Journal of Theology and Philosophy*, 2, 3 (Sept. 1981), pp.85–96.
9. Yair Auron's study of Israeli understandings of the Armenian genocide is an exception. Yair Auron, *The Banality of Indifference: Zionism and the Armenian Genocide* (New Brunswick, NJ: Transaction, 2000); Yair Auron, 'The Holocaust and the Israeli Teacher', *Holocaust and Genocide Studies*, 8, 2 (1994), p.225.
10. Hilene Flanzbaum (ed.), *The Americanization of the Holocaust* (London: Johns Hopkins University Press, 1999); Omer Bartov, *Murder in our Midst: The Holocaust, Industrial Killing, and Representation* (New York: Oxford University Press, 1996);

Alvin Rosenfeld, 'The Americanization of the Holocaust', *Commentary*, 99 (June 1995), pp.35–40; Berenbaum, *AfterTragedy*.

11. Ibid. See also Stephen Katz, *The Holocaust in Historical Context*, vol. 1, *The Holocaust and Mass Death before the Modern Age* (New York: Oxford University Press, 1994).

12. Berenbaum, 'The Uniqueness and Universality of the Holocaust'; Berenbaum, *After Tragedy*, pp.3–16, 20, 33–42.

13. Berenbaum, 'The Uniqueness and Universality of the Holocaust'; see also Berenbaum, cited in Linenthal, *Preserving Memory*, pp.44–5.

14. Alvin H. Rosenfeld, 'The Americanization of the Holocaust', *Commentary*, 99 (June 1995), pp.35–40.

15. Alvin H. Rosenfeld, 'The Holocaust in Jewish Memory and Public Memory', *Dimensions*, 2, 3 (1986), pp.9–12.

16. Ibid.

17. Peter Novick, *The Holocaust in American Life* (New York: Houghton Mifflin, 1999).

18. Tim Cole, *Selling the Holocaust: From Auschwitz to Schindler: How History is Bought, Packaged and Sold* (New York: Routledge, 1999).

19. Norman Finkelstein, *The Holocaust Industry: Reflections on the Exploitation of Jewish Suffering* (New York: Verso, 2000).

20. Tom Segev, *The Seventh Million: The Israelis and the Holocaust* (New York: Hill & Wang, 1993).

21. Tony Kushner, *The Holocaust and the Liberal Imagination* (Oxford: Blackwell, 1994); Franklin Bialystok, *Delayed Impact: The Holocaust and the Canadian Jewish Community* (London: McGill-Queen's University Press, 2000); Judith E. Berman, *Holocaust Remembrance in Australian Jewish Communities, 1945–2000* (Perth: University of Western Australia Press, 2001).

22. David S. Wyman, (ed.), *The World Reacts to the Holocaust* (Baltimore, MD: Johns Hopkins University Press, 1996).

23. Judith Miller, *One, by One, by One: Facing the Holocaust* (London: Simon & Schuster, 1990).

24. Suzanne Rutland, *Edge of the Diaspora: Two Centuries of Jewish Settlement in Australia* (Sydney: Collins Australia, 1988).

25. Alana Rosenbaum, 'Immigrants boost Kiwi community', *AJN (Melb.)*, 22 March 2002, p.5. According to the 2001 New Zealand Census, there are 7,296 Jews in New Zealand, with the majority in Auckland, 1,200 in Wellington and 650 in Christchurch. Of course, the census figures do not reflect Jews unknown to the organized community's leadership.

26. W.D. Rubinstein, *The Jews in Australia: A Thematic History* (Melbourne: William Heinemann, 1991), vol.II, pp.36–7.

27. Ibid., p.69.

28. Ibid., p.77.

29. Colin Golvan, *The Distant Exodus* (Sydney: ABC Enterprises for the Australian Broadcasting Corporation, 1990), p.9. See also, Suzanne Rutland, 'Historical Background (2): 1933–1967', in S. Encel and B. Buckley (eds.), *The New South Wales Jewish Community: A Survey*, 2nd edn (Sydney: New South Wales University Press, 1978), p.23.

30. As Bill Rubinstein has pointed out, since the early 1950s, Australian Jewry was 'inward-looking, concerned almost solely with its own future, with Jewish issues and an exclusively Jewish agenda', Rubinstein, *Jews in Australia*, vol.II, p.6.

31. W.D. Rubinstein, *A History of the Jews in the English-Speaking World: Great Britain* (London: Macmillan, 1996).

32. Tony Kushner, 'Holocaust Survivors in Britain: An Overview and Research Agenda', *Journal of Holocaust Education*, 4, 2 (1995), pp.155–6.

33. Kushner, *Holocaust and the Liberal Imagination*; Anne Beaglehole and Hal Levine, *Far*

From the Promised Land: Being Jewish in New Zealand (Wellington: Pacific Press, 1995).

34. For example, Australian Jewry publicly protested against the post-war migration of Germans to Australia.

35. For a more detailed discussion of multiculturalism in Australia, see Stephen S. Castles, 'Australian Multiculturalism: Social Policy and Identity in a Changing Society', in Gary P. Freeman and James Jupp (eds.), *Nations of Immigrants: Australia, the United States, and International Migration* (Oxford: Oxford University Press, 1992), pp.184–201.

36. New Zealand has never adopted multiculturalism as official policy. New Zealand's predominantly bicultural society is less inclusive of the cultural heritage of non-Christians and non-Europeans. As Beaglehole and Levine point out, 'Jews in New Zealand are pakeha like everyone else with white skin', *Far From the Promised Land*, p.141.

37. Bill Rubinstein, personal communication, 29 July 2003. These figures are disputed. According to Chief Rabbi Sir Jonathan Sacks, the Jewish population has declined by 50 per cent since the 1950s; Jonathan Sacks, 'From Integration to Survival to Continuity: The Third Great Era of Modern Jewry', in Jonathan Webber (ed.), *Jewish Identities in the New Europe* (London: Littman Library of Jewish Civilisation: Oxford Centre for Hebrew and Jewish Studies, 1994), p.112. According to statistics gathered by the Board of Deputies of British Jews, 'by the 1990s British Jewry was approximately one-third smaller than it had been in 1950': www.bod.org.uk/community_stats.shtml accessed 16 Feb. 2002.

38. Rubinstein, *History of the Jews in the English-Speaking World*, pp.418–19. Experts have suggested to Rubinstein that the intermarriage rate in Britain is about 33 per cent.

39. Rosenbaum, 'Immigrants boost Kiwi community', p.5. However, New Zealand Jewry has recently increased in size, attributed to young families arriving, mostly to Auckland, from South Africa, and to a lesser and extent Israel.

40. Beaglehole and Levine, *Far From the Promised Land*, p.139.

41. See Barry A. Kosmin, 'Localism and Pluralism in British Jewry 1900–80', *Transactions of the Jewish Historical Society of England*, 1 (1984), p.120; Geoffrey Alderman, 'British Jewry: An Ethnic Minority?', in Webber (ed.), *Jewish Identities in the New Europe* (London: Littman Library of Jewish Civilisation, Oxford Centre for Hebrew and Jewish Studies, 1994), p.191; Geoffrey Alderman, *Modern British Jewry* (Oxford: Oxford University Press, 1992), p.378. Livia Kathe Wittman, *International Identities: Jewish Women in New Zealand* (Palmerston North: Dunmore, 1988), p.36.

42. The *New Zealand Jewish Chronicle* reaches the homes of about 75 per cent of the country's Jews; Stephen Levine, *The New Zealand Jewish Community*, New York, p. 133.

43. The *Jewish Chronicle*, with sales of over 50,000 copies a week, is the largest and most influential national institution in British Jewry; Kosmin, 'Localism and pluralism', p. 119.

44. Michel Foucault, 'Nietzsche, Genealogy, History', in Donald F. Bouchard (ed.), *Language, Counter-Memory, Practice: Selected Essays and Interviews* (Ithica, NY: Cornell University Press, 1997).

45. The terms social memory and collective memory will be used interchangeably in this book.

46. See Nathan Wachtell, Introduction to special issue 'Between Memory and History', *History and Anthropology*, 2 (1986), pp.211–17.

47. Eric Hobsbawm and T. Ranger (eds.), *The Invention of Tradition* (Cambridge: Cambridge University Press, 1983); Benedict Anderson, *Imagined Communities: Reflections on the Origin and Spread of Nationalism* (London: Verso, 1991).

CHAPTER 2

1. For example, see Rochelle Saidel, *Never Too Late to Remember: The Politics Behind New York City's Holocaust Museum* (London: Holmes & Meier, 1996), pp.30–4.
2. Peter Novick, *The Holocaust in American Life* (New York: Houghton Mifflin, 1999), p.152.
3. Ibid.
4. *NZJC*, May 1961, p.5.
5. The main centre of the Jewish population in Britain is Greater London and the contiguous counties, which comprises 72 per cent of British Jewry. For this reason, this book concentrates on Holocaust remembrance activities in London. However, it should be noted that Holocaust memorialization also took place in Glasgow, Manchester, Leeds, Dublin, Birmingham and other areas where significant numbers of Jews resided.
6. Non-Orthodox congregations in Britain – the Union of Liberal and Progressive Synagogues, and the Assembly of Reform Ministers – supported the choice of 27th Nissan; 'Dispute over date for remembrance day', *JC*, 15 April 1966, pp.1, 12.
7. The situation was different in New Zealand where services usually took place in synagogues and were lead by Rabbis.
8. Of course there were exceptions to this generalization. For example, Rabbi Chaim Gutnick in Melbourne, and Rabbi Gotschall in Sydney were actively involved in Holocaust memorialization. Rabbi Gotschall (and from 1978 by Rev. Michael Deutch) gathered together former residents of Czechoslovakia each year from March 1950 to commemorate the destruction of Czechoslovakian Jewry.
9. Letter from David Carrington, Press and PR Officer to Mr Silverman, Secretary of the United Synagogue, 1 Feb. 1963; Letter from United Synagogue's head office in Woburn House to Mr Carrington, Press and Public Relations officer of the Board of Deputies, 28 Feb. 1963, ACC/3121/C8/2/31, Board of Deputies' Archive (BDA). Indeed, it has been pointed out that in Britain *Yom haShoah* has been 'treated with curious ambivalence by the religious establishment'; 'Forgetting to Remember', *New Moon* (June 1992).
10. The commemorations at Carlton were organized by the Katzetler Farband which, in the early 1960s, widened its membership and changed its name to the Association of Jewish Victims of Nazi Persecution (although the organization is still frequently referred to by its original title). The Rookwood memorial was initiated by the NSW Board and erected by the Jewish Cemetery Trust and the Sydney Chevra Kadisha; see Hans Kimmel (Dr Joseph Steadtler), *Sydney's Jewish Community: Materials for a Post-War (II) History, 1951–1953* (Sydney: n.p., 1955), p.200. The annual commemorative services at Carlton and Rookwood, attended mainly by survivors, are shorter and more emotional than the main Jewish community *Yom haShoah* commemoration. The main *Yom haShoah* commemorations were complemented by a variety of other annual Holocaust commemorations organized by *landsmanschaften*, the Bund, the Folk Centre and other refugee and survivor organizations in Melbourne and Sydney. The small size of the pre-war and post-war Jewish refugee intake into Western Australia meant that for over forty years the annual *Yom haShoah* commemoration remained the only institutionalized public form of Holocaust remembrance.
11. The Board of Deputies of British Jews, established in 1760, is the 'official' lay representative body of British Jewry. Over the past fifty years, as Anglo-Jewry has become more fragmented, the influence of the Board has declined and it has become one of a number of Jewish leadership elites.
12. For example, at the 1959 commemoration, Dr S. Levenberg, the London representative of the Jewish Agency asked: 'Where are the official representatives

of English Jewry?'; Dr S. Levenberg, quoted in 'Warsaw Ghetto Heroes Remembered', *JC*, 24 April 1959, p.5.

13. Established in the early 1960s, the Memorial Committee, dominated by Jewish socialists and sponsored mainly by prominent British Jews as well as some non-Jewish parliamentarians, aimed to establish 'a permanent memorial to the heroes of the WGU; the six million Jewish and millions of other victims of Nazism'; 'Ghetto Memorial Fund Launched', *JC*, 24 May 1963, p.12; also Memorial Committee, ACC/3121/C10/5/04, BDA.

14. Law, Parliamentary and General Purpose Committee report, Board of Deputies of British Jews Annual Report, 1960, p.36, BDA.

15. The exhibition, based mainly on material collected and preserved by Dr Alexander Bernfes, a Polish Jew, complemented commemoration of the Warsaw Ghetto Uprising. The exhibition which attracted more than 10,000 visitors over ten days at its first location in the West End of London, aimed to depict, by photos, documents, paintings and relics, the fate and suffering of the Jews in Poland under Nazism.

16. Executive Committee Meeting, 10 April 1962, ACC/3121/C8/2/31, BDA.

17. I am grateful to Bill Rubinstein for these insights.

18. Tony Kushner, *The Holocaust and the Liberal Imagination* (Oxford: Blackwell, 1994).

19. Efforts of the United States and the West to integrate West Germany as an ally in the Cold War against the allegedly aggressive Soviet Union stirred widespread Jewish fear of German re-Nazification.

20. Systematic historical research about the Holocaust, stimulated by the Eichmann Trial, was in its early stages in the 1960s.

21. Peter Wertheim, 'Shadows Amid The Sunshine: A Second Generation Perspective On Growing Up In Australia', *Zachor: The Australian Association of Jewish Holocaust Survivors and Descendants' Journal*, (April 2002), p.26. See also Michael Berenbaum, *After Tragedy and Triumph: Essays on Modern Jewish Thought and the American Experience* (Cambridge: Cambridge University Press, 1991), p.xix.

22. See Ronald Taft, 'The impact of the Middle East crisis of June 1967 on Jews in Melbourne', in Peter Medding (ed.), *Jews in Australian Society* (Melbourne: Macmillan, 1973), pp.123–4. Ronald Taft was Professor of Social Psychology at Monash University.

23. Jonathan Sacks, 'From Integration to Survival to Continuity: The Third Great Era of Modern Jewry', in Jonathan Webber (ed), *Jewish Identities in the New Europe* (London: Littman Library of Jewish Civilisation: Oxford Centre for Hebrew and Jewish Studies, 1994), p.109. Moreover, the reflected glory of Israel's military victories left Jews with renewed self-respect.

24. Grant Noble and Craig Osmond, '"Holocaust" in Australia', *International Journal of Political Education*, 4 (May 1981), pp.139–50. *Holocaust* attracted an audience of 120 million when it was telecast in the United States in 1978; 'Holocaust', *Australian Jewish Times* (hereafter *AJT*), 22 June 1978, p.13.

25. Martin Jackson, 'How many people watched Holocaust?', *Daily Mail*, 12 July 1978.

26. Paul Smith, 'Holocaust: The survivors' final verdict', *Evening News*, 7 Sept. 1978, p.8.

27. Helen Paske, 'Life after the Holocaust', *New Zealand Listener*, 16 June 1979, p.14.

28. Sam Lipski, 'A truly final word', *AJN (Melb.)*, 24 June 1994, p.26.

29. For more about Soviet anti-Semitism and Holocaust denial, see Zvi Gitelman, 'The Soviet Union', in Wyman, *The World Reacts* (Baltimore, MD: Johns Hopkins University Press), pp.316–21.

30. For the history, motivation, tactics and methods of Holocaust deniers, see Deborah E. Lipstadt, *Denying the Holocaust: The Growing Assault on Truth and Memory* (London: Plume, 1994).

31. For more about the relations between Maori and Pakeha in New Zealand see Michael King, *Being Pakeha: An Encounter with New Zealand and the Maori Renaissance*, (Auckland: Penguin: 1985).

32. The 1985 commemoration was officially organized by The New Zealand Jewish Council, in conjunction with the National Council of Churches, and the Mayors of New Zealand's four main centres and Television New Zealand's Credo production team.

33. Jeff Durkin, personal communication, 2 July 2003.

34. Other aspects of the three-hour visit organized by the NCJW include an Israel experience (food tasting and Israeli dancing), and a tour of the synagogue together with explanations about Jewish festivals, traditions and religious practices.

35. *NZJC*, May 1991, p.27. The book was installed in the foyer of Wellington's Orthodox synagogue in 1991 by *B'nai B'rith* and the New Zealand Council of Jewish Women (NCJW).

36. The exhibition consists of photographs, money from a ghetto, identification papers, yellow stars worn by Jews in Europe and a concentration camp uniform. In the late 1990s, three drawings from the Terezin exhibition were added.

37. Museums Company, 'Children of the Holocaust: drawings from Terezin concentration camp, Summary 1998 Tour Report'. Another low profile Holocaust remembrance project in Wellington was the 1992 consecration of a Holocaust Memorial Stone at Makara Cemetery.

38. Holocaust survivor, Sol Filler, was interviewed over the years by various media and he was on the guest speaker circuit to schools, rotary and probus groups.

39. This was made possible by non-Jewish stonemasons and monumental masons who contributed about $8,000. Ruth Filler, personal communication, Dec. 2001.

40. Freda Narev, personal communication, Dec. 2001.

41. Mike Regan, 'Oral Archives', *NZJC*, March 2003, p.17; Mike Regan, 'Auckland home for testimonies', *NZJC*, June 2003, p.13. In 2003 the tapes were presented to the Auckland War Memorial Museum where they will be used as an educational resource.

42. The Armoury Room in the War Memorial, which houses Auckland's Holocaust Oral Archive Group's videos of the testimonies of Holocaust survivors, is used for study and resource purposes.

43. This assertion is confirmed by Anne Beaglehole and Hal Levine, *Far From the Promised Land: Being Jewish in New Zealand* (Wellington: Pacific Press, 1995), p.97. The 1985 commemoration in Wellington was an exception to the rule.

44. Ruth Filler, personal communication, Dec. 2001. Beaglehole and Levine, *Far From the Promised Land*, pp.64, 92–5

45. I thank Andrew Blitz for this insight.

46. The thesis shared many of David Irving's conclusions. The NZJCO requested that the award be revoked. An independent working party subsequently set up by the university criticized Dr Hayward, his research, thesis and conclusions, his supervision and external examiners' reports, but could not find any systematic intention to be dishonest and therefore did not revoke the degree or withdraw the thesis.

47. New Zealand's Jewish community was again affronted when in 2000 Waikato University insensitively allowed a German PhD student, Hans-Joachim Kupka, a former far-right party leader in Bavaria and a Holocaust denier, to enrol to undertake a thesis in which he would interview Holocaust survivors without their being aware of his far right-wing views; Mike Regan, 'Gould apology over New Zealand dispute', *JC*, 18 Oct. 2002, p.14; Allon Lee, 'NZ uni apologises to Jews', *AJN (Melb.)*, 18 Oct. 2002, p.9; Deborah Stone, 'NZ Holocaust denial inquiry', *AJN (Melb.)*, 18 Aug. 2000, p.3.

48. For a more detailed discussion of multiculturalism in Australia, see Stephen S. Castles, 'Australian Multiculturalism: Social Policy and Identity in a Changing Society', in Gary P. Freeman and James Jupp (eds), *Nations of Immigrants: Australia, the United States, and International Migration* (Oxford: Oxford University Press, 1992), pp.184–201.

49. Suzanne Rutland, *Edge of the Diaspora: Two Centuries of Jewish Settlement in Australia* (Sydney: Collins Australia, 1988), p.369.

50. *B'nai B'rith*, meaning 'Sons of the Covenant', is an international fraternal society which was founded in New York City in 1843. *B'nai B'rith* is dedicated to education, tolerance, harmony and social justice, focusing on a wide range of community service projects, directed at enhancing inter-communal understanding and tolerance.

51. The Association of Ex-Victims of Nazi Persecution, the Federation of Polish Jews, *Kadimah*, and the Community Assistants Group all contributed to the exhibition. Allan Nahum, quoted in 'Holocaust Memories', *AJN*, 8 Feb. 1980, p.7.

52. Eric Butler and the Australian League of Rights (an extreme right-wing group) denied German persecution of the Jews during the Second World War, and from the 1950s referred to the 'myth' of the six million Jewish victims of Nazism as a propaganda hoax. Since 1979 John Bennett, lawyer and secretary of the Victorian Council for Civil Liberties, has been a major proponent of Holocaust denial in Australia; Hilary Rubinstein, 'Dating Holocaust denial', *AJN (Melb.)*, 9 Dec. 1994, p.38. Most recent Holocaust denialists in Australia have been Adelaide-based, such as Dr Fredrick Toben and Tasmanian Olga Scully. In 2002 Toben received a Federal Court order to remove all matter denying the Holocaust from his Adelaide Institute website and Scully was ordered by the Federal Court to stop disseminating anti-Semitic literature; Allon Lee, 'Purge internet hate, court orders Toben', *AJN (Melb.)*, 20 Sept. 2002, p.1. For more about the history of Holocaust denial in Australia see Hilary Rubinstein, 'Early Manifestations of Holocaust Denial in Australia', *Australian Jewish Historical Society Journal*, 14, 1 (1997), pp.93–109.

53. Joe Gersh, Report of the Honorary Secretary, *Annual Report of the Victorian Jewish Board of Deputies, 1979/80*, p.11.

54. Allan Nahum, quoted in 'Holocaust Memories', *AJN*, 8 Feb. 1980, p.7.

55. The organizers were not disappointed with the response of the general community: 7,500 people in Melbourne, including 2,500 school children from thirty-nine schools, viewed the 1980 Holocaust Exhibition; Avraham Zeleznikow, Report of the Chairman of the Jewish Heritage Committee, *Annual Report of the Victorian Jewish Board of Deputies, 1979/80*, p.37.

56. Ibid., p.38; Avraham Zeleznikow, Report of the Chairman of the Jewish Heritage Committee, *Annual Report of the Victorian Jewish Board of Deputies, 1981*, p.48.

57. Bono Wiener and Shmuel Rosenkranz, 'Our Work Is Even More Important Now', in Stan Marks (ed.), *10 Years: Jewish Holocaust Museum and Research Centre, Melbourne, 1984–94* (Melbourne: Jewish Holocaust Museum and Research Centre, 1994), pp.11–12.

58. After surviving the Holocaust, Aron Sokolowicz emigrated to Australia and became President of the Federation of Polish Jews and member of the *Kadimah*. Sokolowicz died in 1991. Bono Wiener, also a Holocaust survivor, was a *Bundist* leader, *Kadimah* stalwart, co-founder of *Sholem Aleichem Yiddish* school, and Australian Labour Party activist till his death in 1995.

59. Wiener hid two boxes of documents in the Lodz ghetto; see Matthew Ricketson, 'Holocaust remembered to celebrate freedom', *Weekend Australian*, 28–29 May 1988, p.8.

60. Helen Light, 'Holocaust Museums and Memorials', unpublished manuscript, May 1995, p.13.

61. Saba Feniger, 'Tell The World All About It', *Centre News*, 6, 1 (March 1989), p.9.
62. Kitia Altman, quoted in Eva Friedman, 'A voice for survivors', *AJN (Melb.)*, 24 June 1994, life/style p.8. Altman wrote this after her 1993 satellite confrontation with David Irving on Channel Nine's *A Current Affair*, a television prime-time programme. In 1987 the Australian League of Rights had sponsored a visit to Australia by David Irving. Although Irving's plans to conduct additional lecture tours of Australia have been curtailed by denials of a visa, each application evokes Holocaust memories in survivors.
63. Phillip Maisel, coordinator of the project since 1994, has to date recorded the testimonies of over 1,200 survivors on videotape.
64. The MHMandRC, together with the Jewish Museum in Melbourne and the Raoul Wallenberg Unit of *B'nai Brith*, has been integral to the development and success of the travelling Courage to Care exhibition. For more, see chapter six.
65. Stan Marks, 'Experiment Could Help Prevent Offenders', *Centre News*, 21, 3 (Dec. 2002), p.2.
66. Wiener and Rosenkranz, 'Our Work Is Even More Important Now', p.11.
67. Photos of some of the posters appeared in *Maccabean*, 24 June 1988. In 1990 Jack van Tongeren, the leader of the organization, was convicted of fire-bombing a number of Chinese restaurants and was jailed for eighteen years. Co-conspirators Chris Bartle and Wayne and John van Blitterswyck were jailed for shorter periods.
68. Brendan Nicholson, 'Scarred For Life'. *West Australian*, 'Big Weekend', 29 June 1991, p.1.
69. Ben Korman, Director of the Holocaust Institute of WA, explained that 'Many of the survivors have kept their stories bottled up. But they hear these denials of the Holocaust, they know they will not live forever and they have to tell'; Ben Korman, quoted ibid., p.2.
70. Conversations with guides of the Holocaust Institute of WA, 1995–2000. In 1990 three survivors and five guides worked at the Institute; by 2003 the numbers had increased to nine survivors and eleven guides.
71. For example, in June 1993 the Institute organized the display of the *Courage to Care: Rescuers of Jews During the Holocaust* exhibition at the Western Australian Museum and in 2000 survivors and guides from the Holocaust Institute played an integral role with the travelling Courage to Care/Anne Frank exhibition.
72. Including, among others, Arnold Zable, Therkel Straede, Yitzchak Kerem, Jonathan Steinberg and Yehuda Bauer.
73. It is the first Holocaust memorial to be built in public space in Australia.
74. 'Sydney public reaction to Holocaust Exhibition', *AJT*, 23 July 1981, p.4.
75. 'Holocaust Association sets membership "goal"', *AJT*, 14 April 1983, p.8; 'Holocaust group formed in Sydney', *AJT*, 13 Jan. 1983, p.4. The Constitution of Sydney's AJHS listed among its aims and objectives: 'to assist in acquiring and maintaining a premises as a permanent museum of artefacts and memorabilia from the Holocaust period'; Constitution of the Australian Association of Jewish Holocaust Survivors (head office, Sydney), Aims and Objectives, no.3 k.
76. Alex Gottshall, 'Impact Meet On Holocaust', *AJN*, 8 March 1985.
77. Albert Halm, quoted in 'Survivors Plan Commemoration', *AJT*, 23 Feb. 1984, p.10.
78. Albert Halm (ed.), *The Gift of Life: A Commemorative Book of the Holocaust Gathering, May 1985* (Sydney: Australian Association of Jewish Holocaust Survivors, 1988), p.13. For more information about the League of Right's exhibition in Adelaide, see W.D. Rubinstein, *The Jews in Australia: A Thematic History* (Melbourne: William Heinemann, 1991), II, 461.
79. The three-day academic programme of workshops, seminars and lectures was accompanied by a small, condensed version of the 1981 Exhibition, arranged by Sylvia Rosenblum, curator of the A.M. Rosenblum Jewish Museum in the Great

Synagogue, and displayed under the title 'This Really Did Happen'.

80. Albert Halm, 'Summation of the Holocaust Gathering in Sydney, May 1985', *News Digest* (1985), pp.8–10. Few Australian-born Jews took part in the gathering.

81. Ibid., p.8. The Association of Jewish Holocaust Survivors (AJHS) was soon after renamed the Australian Association of Jewish Holocaust Survivors (AAJHS). In 1994 the organization changed its name to Australian Association of Jewish Holocaust Survivors and Descendants (AAJHS&D), after incorporating the Second Generation group.

82. The task of cataloguing Holocaust memorabilia held by survivors in Sydney had initially been undertaken by Rabbi Alfred Fabian; see 'Holocaust Association sets membership "goal"', *AJT*, 14 April 1983, p.8.

83. The museum committee was established as a sub-committee of the Association of Jewish Holocaust Survivors. Exhibitions included 'We Are Here – Images of the Holocaust' (1987), 'A Question of Survival' (1989), and 'A Generation Lost' (1991). Some of the photos from these exhibitions were later enlarged and became part of the permanent exhibition of the Sydney Jewish Museum.

84. John Engelman, Report of the President of the Australian Association of Jewish Holocaust Survivors, *News Digest* (April 1989). Eliezer Wiesel is a world-renowned novelist, philosopher, humanitarian, political activist and Holocaust survivor. He is the author of over 40 books, the most famous of which, *Night*, describes his experiences during the Holocaust. Yisrael Gutman is a world-renowned Holocaust historian.

85. John Roth, Sydney Jewish Museum membership renewal letter, 21 May 2002.

86. The Australian Institute of Holocaust Studies was founded in 1986 under the auspices of the NSW Board of Deputies by high profile members of the Jewish community and Holocaust survivors who intended that it would become the Sydney Centre for documentation, teaching, research and information on the Holocaust and anti-Semitism. The Institute was never particularly active and the Sydney Jewish Museum and the AAJHS took over many of its intended roles.

87. It had been Saunder's wish that the Sydney Jewish community would eventually shoulder the financial burden of the Sydney Jewish museum. The museum received a generous bequest by the late John Saunders of $2 million, plus a commitment of the Prime Minister, John Howard, of a donation by the Australian Government of $1 million.

88. 'A Museum of Remembrance', *AJN*, 15 April 1988, p.10.

89. 'Holocaust Centre a "living museum"', *AJT*, 8 May 1986, p.13.

90. 'Holocaust Museum venue for Vic. Board meeting', *AJT*, 17 April 1986, p.9.

91. Anon., Holocaust Centre volunteer, personal communication, 21 Nov. 1995. For the most recent example, see Shmuel Rosenkranz, 'Community Effort Needed To Keep Holocaust Centre Alive', *Centre News*, 14, 1 (April 1997), p.2. Rosenkranz asserted that 'our Centre is better known, and its work seemingly even better appreciated, by the non-Jewish community than the Jewish community'.

92. For a comprehensive history of Holocaust education at Australian Jewish high schools see Judith E. Berman, *Holocaust Remembrance in Australian Jewish Communities, 1945–2000* (Perth: University of Western Australia Press, 2001). The first course about the Holocaust to be offered at an Australian university was Konrad Kwiet's 'The Persecution and Destruction of European Jewry 1933–45', which was taught in the German Studies department of the University of NSW for most of the years between 1977 and 1992. This course alternated for some years with Kwiet's 'Emancipation, Antisemitism and Zionism'. Kwiet has also taught 'From the Enlightenment to the Nazi Era', 'The German-Jewish Experience' and 'Germany after 1945'. Courses about the Holocaust have since been taught at many other Australian universities.

93. 'For Jews to solidify the place of the Holocaust within Jewish consciousness they must establish its importance for the American people as a whole'; Berenbaum, *After Tragedy and Triumph*, p.16.

94. Kushner, *Holocaust and the Liberal Imagination*, p.261.

95. Letter from Dan Jones to Greville Janner, MP, 1 Feb. 1982, YVCUK correspondence file, 1982–85, ACC/3121/E4/912, BDA.

96. YVCUK minutes, 12 July 1982; 9 Dec. 1982, ACC/3121/C23/01/01, BDA.

97. Martin Sugarman, letter to the editor, 'Fate of teaching pack', *JC*, 10 June 1988, p.25.

98. Kushner, *Holocaust and the Liberal Imagination*, pp.261–2.

99. YVCUK, which had been established in 1976, was intended as a support committee in Britain for *Yad Vashem* in Israel but soon became incorporated into the Board and focused on education, commemoration and memorialization of the Holocaust in Britain. Educational material included a pamphlet, 'The facts about the destruction of European Jewry by the Nazis', Martin Gilbert's *The Holocaust: Maps and Photographs*, and films.

100. The claim that Zionists collaborated with the Nazis in carrying out the Holocaust were common among Marxists in Britain in the 1970s and 1980s. Holocaust denial in the 1980s was linked to a range of national and international ultra right parties and groups; W.D. Rubinstein, *Jews in the English-Speaking World: Great Britain* (London: Macmillan, 1996), pp.377, 382–4.

101. Simon Freeman and Patrick Bishop, 'Holocaust – truth behind the schmaltz', *Evening Standard*, 6 Sept. 1978, p.3. See also, Hugo Gryn with Naomi Gryn, *Chasing Shadows* (London: Viking, 2000), p.247.

102. Kitty Hart, *Return to Auschwitz* (London: Sidgwick & Jackson, 1981), p.23. The television film *Kitty Returns to Auschwitz* (1979) was made with the explicit intention of countering Holocaust denial.

103. Rubinstein, *Jews in the English-Speaking World*, pp.28–35. As a new generation of Anglo-Jews arose, previous, distinct but also positive, perceptions of Anglo-Jewish identity were collapsing.

104. Suzanne Bardgett, 'The Genesis and Development of the Imperial War Museum's Holocaust Exhibition Project', *Journal of Holocaust Education*, 7, 3 (Winter 1998), pp.29–30. Interest in the small 'Belsen 1945' exhibition which was displayed at the Imperial War Museum (IWM) from 1991, and the IWM's re-evaluation of its mission, contributed to this decision.

105. Ben Helfgott, personal communication, Oct. 2000.

106. 'Timely proposal', *JC*, 18 Nov. 1994, p.26. In the mid 1990s the London Museum of Jewish Life had allocated space in a new building for a Holocaust education gallery but, according to the museum's chairman of trustees, 'the response to our appeal for funds for this project was disappointing'; 'Holocaust museum', letters to the editor, *JC*, 9 Sept. 1994, p.19.

107. Ronnie Landau, 'Holocaust museum', letter to editor, *JC*, 25 Nov. 1994, p.22; See also, Edgar Samuel (Director of the Jewish Museum), letter to editor, ibid. Similarly, Simon Rocker asserted, 'For many, the most attractive proposition is the Imperial War Museum's [proposal] precisely because it is a national and not a Jewish institution'; Simon Rocker, 'Remembrance or renewal', *JC*, 2 Dec. 1994, p.29.

108. Simon Rocker, 'Holocaust centre in net growth on fifth birthday', *JC*, 3 Nov. 2000, p.13.

109. In 1996 the Anglo-Jewish Ex-Servicemen's Association (AJEX) had taken a lead in approaching MPs with a view to the establishment of a Holocaust Memorial Day in Britain; YVCUK minutes, 13 March 1996, 1994–2000 file, BDA.

110. The Home Office's Consultation Paper was produced by a small working group chaired by the Home Office and including representatives of the Holocaust

Education Trust (HET), Anne Frank Educational Trust, Beth Shalom Holocaust Memorial Centre, Board of Deputies of British Jews, London Borough of Barnet and officials from the Foreign and Commonwealth Office, Department of Culture, Media and Sport, and the Department of Education and Employment.

111. This date coincided with remembrance days in Germany and Sweden, and fell in line with the European Union's Genocide Remembrance Day. For more about the Stockholm Conference, HMD and the International Task Force, see www.holocaustforum.gov.se; www.holocaustmemorialday.gov.uk; http://taskforce.ushmm.gov.

112. Of course, the establishment of Holocaust Memorial Day does not mean that Britain has become more multicultural and tolerant.

113. In 2000 the Holocaust received widespread media coverage when Holocaust denier David Irving sued American academic Deborah Lipstadt and her British publisher for libel, claiming that *Denying the Holocaust* defamed him by stating that he had distorted, manipulated and falsified history. For more about the trial see Richard J. Evans, *Lying About Hitler: History, Holocaust and the David Irving Trial* (London: Basic, 2002).

114. Yehuda Bauer, 'We are condemned to remember', *Jerusalem Post*, 19 April 2001.

115. The announcement by Barnett Janner, at the 1969 Warsaw Ghetto Uprising commemoration, that a Holocaust library and commemorative hall would be included in the proposed Jewish community centre in London was perceived by the author of a *JC* editorial as 'inadequate and inappropriate ... Whether intended or not the utilisation of the hallowed memory of the martyrs to raise funds for a worthy but unrelated cause smack of gimmickry'. 'Memorial Project', *JC*, 18 April 1969, p.8.

116. Cyla Sokolowicz, 'Editorial', *Centre News*, 6, 2 (June 1989), p.3.

CHAPTER 3

1. Michael Berenbaum, *After Tragedy and Triumph: Modern Jewish Thought and the American Experience* (New York: Cambridge University Press, 1990). Berenbaum resigned in 1980 and returned in 1987 to become Project Director. In 1993 Berenbaum became Director of the Research Institute.

2. Arguably, in an age of globalization, there is little difference between the so-called 'American' values conveyed in the United States Holocaust Memorial Museum and Australian, British, New Zealand or Western ideals and values. Thus, if the Holocaust has been reshaped in accordance with Australian, British and New Zealand ideals, values and historical experiences, it will have been 'universalized' rather than 'Australianized', 'Anglicized' or 'Kiwized'.

3. Michael Berenbaum, 'The Americanization of the Holocaust', in Ilya Lekov (ed.), *Bitburg and Beyond* (New York: Shapolsky, 1987), p.709.

4. Alvin H. Rosenfeld, 'The Americanization of the Holocaust', *Commentary*, 99 (June 1995), p.36.

5. Ibid., p.35.

6. Henryk Grynberg, 'Appropriating the Holocaust', *Commentary*, 74 (Nov. 1982), p.57.

7. More recently, Yehuda Bauer has referred to the 'unprecedented' nature of the Holocaust; Yehuda Bauer, *Rethinking the Holocaust* (New Haven, CT: Yale University Press, 2001).

8. Rabbi Irving Greenberg, *The Jewish Way: Living the Holidays* (New York, 1988), p.342. Similarly, Ronnie Landau has asserted that in order to avoid its marginalization, the Holocaust should be integrated into general historical inquiry

and presented as of universal, and not purely Jewish, significance; Simon Rocker, 'School teachers shun Holocaust', in ibid. Alan Jacobs too argues that 'Comparing and contrasting the Holocaust will surely keep it a valuable comparative frame of reference': Alan Jacobs, 'The Holocaust and Comparative Genocide: Paradigms in Conflict?', *ITN Network: Journal of the Australian Institute for Holocaust and Genocide Studies*, 15, 1–2 (July 2001), p.5.

9.   Berenbaum, *After Tragedy*, p.22.

10.   Rabbi Silberman, paraphrased in *NZJC*, 4 May 1964, p.11. See also 'Ghetto martyrs remembered', *JC*, 4 May 1962, p.11.

11.   Commemorations of the Holocaust in Diaspora communities were affected by post-war developments in the State of Israel where the alleged passive behaviour of European Jewry in the Holocaust was considered shameful by Israelis still fighting for the survival of their vulnerable state. This depiction of the victims as having not resisted or defended themselves reflected early statist Zionist ideology and its inherent 'negation of the Diaspora' in which the Holocaust symbolized exile, and Israel the redemption of the Jewish people. Although only a few instances of physical resistance were known at the time, heroism, as in Jewish physical resistance to Nazism, was over emphasized because it was perceived by the founding fathers of Israel as the one feature from the Holocaust experience that the 'new Israeli Jews' could both identify with and respect.

12.   The source of this oft repeated phrase is Chaim Nahman Bialik's poem, 'In the city of slaughter', written in the aftermath of the 1903 Kishinev pogrom.

13.   Ben Green, paraphrased in 'The Warsaw Ghetto Revolt Commemoration', *AJN (Melb.)*, 9 May 1947, p.8. Over time other instances of uprisings in concentration camps and ghettos became publicly known, but the Warsaw ghetto revolt, which had a powerful impact especially on Polish pre-war refugees and survivors but also on the wider community, turned into the symbol of all armed Jewish resistance to Nazism.

14.   The trial spurred serious scholarship about the Holocaust. Although early publications tended to reinforce the previously held attitudes of Israelis, systematic historical research about the Holocaust had begun.

15.   For example, see 'Youth Pays Tribute to Heroes', *AJT*, 26 April 1963, p.5.

16.   However, there are unpleasing Jewish experiences of the Holocaust, such as those of collaboration or the alleged lack of assertive responses from some Jewish communities worldwide to the plight of European Jewry under Nazism, which have been 'strategically forgotten'.

17.   For example, see 'London mourns heroes of Uprising', *JC*, 26 April 1963, p.12. For an alternative evaluation of these issues, see William D. Rubinstein, *The Myth of Rescue* (London: Routledge, 1997).

18.   'London mourns heroes of Uprising', *JC*, 26 April 1963, p.12.

19.   Abba Kovner, quoted in 'Youth Told Memorial Reasons', *AJN*, 22 April 1966, p.5.

20.   Dr Geoffrey Levy, quoted in 'Some Thoughts On Jewish Martyrs' Day', *NZJC*, 4 May 1964, p.10. A similar situation was described at Wellington's 1964 commemoration where a speaker also referred to the 'apathy of friendly nations to the sufferings of the Jews in Europe': 'Martyrs' Remembrance Commemoration', ibid, p.11.

21.   'Righteous Among the Nations' is the term designated by *Yad Vashem* to describe a non-Jew who endangered his or her own life to help to rescue a Jew from the Nazi death machine.

22.   Over the last decade the traditional six candles have sometimes represented six destroyed Jewish communities, or the victims of six concentration camps. Occasionally one of the six candles has been designated as representing the non-Jewish victims of Nazism.

23. Pierre Nora, 'Between Memory and History: *Les Lieux de Memoire*', special issue on Memory and Counter Memory, *Representations,* 26 (Spring 1989), p.9.

24. Joe Berinson, quoted in 'Community Divides Over Ghetto Services', *AJN*, 28 April 1972, p.9. Berinson was a Labour Member of the Federal House of Representatives.

25. For example, see Graham de Vahl Davis, quoted in 'Community urged to "fight denial of holocaust"', *AJT*, 17 April 1980, p.3.

26. 'Perth Jewry honours the heroes of the Warsaw Ghetto', *Maccabean*, 4 May 1973, p.1.

27. Isi Leibler, quoted in 'World Share in Jewish Dead', *AJN*, 4 May 1973, p.5. See also, Shalom Grayek, quoted in 'Israeli attacks justified', *JC*, 4 May 1973, p.17.

28. Mr Frisner, quoted in 'Auschwitz mark inspired soldier', *JC*, 30 April 1976, p.7. Simon Frisner, Chairman of PJEX, read these words to the 1976 commemoration in London. According to Frisner's understanding, the Allies' neglect of the fate of the Jews for the follies of appeasement, and in 1973 for the sake of Arab oil, meant that Jews had to guard against anti-Semitism and anti-Zionism; Simon Frisner, 'Silkin warning on scapegoats', *JC*, 11 April 1975, p.5.

29. *NZJC*, April 1951, p.2. At Wellington's 1955 commemoration, M. Kaplan of the Yiddish Circle expressed his concern that twelve years was too short a time for the German people to be cleansed of their guilt; 'In Wellington: The Martyrs Remembered', *NZJC*, May 1955, p.13.

30. Alec Wasserman, quoted in 'Ghetto Rising Rally', *JC*, 16 April 1954, p.9. Similar sentiments were also expressed at a commemoration organized by the Stepney Communist Party that same year; see 'Ghetto Memorial Meeting', *JC*, 9 April 1954, p.11.

31. Rabbi Sanger, quoted in 'Kadimah Commemoration for Warsaw Ghetto', *AJN*, 7 May 1954, p.5; see also 'Seven Hundred Mourn Six Million Dead', *AJN*, 22 April 1955, p.3; 'Ghetto Survivor Hits at Jews who Trade with Germany', *SJN*, 22 April 1955, p.2. Similarly, in London, Zylberberg asserted that it was the duty of every Jew to shun all contact with Germans: 'In Memory of the Warsaw Ghetto', *JC*, 1954, p.8.

32. Ben Green, President of the Executive Council of Australian Jewry, quoted in 'Two Melbourne Meetings Commemorate The Warsaw Ghetto Uprising', *Hebrew Standard*, 27 April 1951, p.3.

33. Germany was the focus of commemorations again in the mid 1960s as protests were aired at the refusal of the West German government to extend the Statute of Limitations on the trial of Nazi war criminals.

34. Colin Schindler suggests that some of the Soviet Jewry activists may be motivated by guilt. 'To some people the campaign is a psychological reaction to the failure to save Jews during the Holocaust. Now they perceive a concrete problem, they want to act.' Quoted in Stephen Brook, *The Club* (London: Constable, 1989), p.364.

35. For about a decade following the end of the Second World War, many speakers at Holocaust commemorations expressed their concerned about the remnant of European Jewry remaining in Displaced Persons camps in Europe. Communities were called upon to donate to the Israel Appeal that would help rescue, assist and rehabilitate the survivors and build Israel as the homeland for those wishing to settle there.

36. Dr Geoffrey Levy, quoted in 'Some Thoughts On Jewish Martyrs' Day', *NZJC*, 4 May 1964, p.10.

37. Rabbi Mattis Kantor, quoted in 'Commemoration warning', *AJT*, 29 April 1971, p.7. Australian Jewry become involved in the plight of Soviet Jewry after Isi Leibler, Public Relations officer of the Victorian Board, had initiated a major campaign in 1962. For more about Australian Jewish involvement in the campaign for Soviet Jewry, see W.D. Rubinstein, *The Jews in Australia: A Thematic History*

(Melbourne: William Heinemann, 1991), II, 437–40.

38.   Concern for increasing anti-Semitism in Poland was first expressed in 1957: *JC*, 12 April 1957, p.10. It should be noted that although rarely expressed in commemorations, the campaign to free Soviet Jewry was a high priority for Anglo Jewry.

39.   'Revival of Holocaust spirit condemned', *JC*, 26 April 1968, p.21.

40.   Ibid.

41.   'Ghetto Martyrs inspire living', *JC*, 29 April 1977, p.7.

42.   'Warsaw martyrs received "no help"', *JC*, 15 May 1981, p.11.

43.   David Winner, 'Tears for heroes', *JC*, 8 May 1987, p.23; David Winner, 'Candles and tears at Hyde Park', *JC*, 5 May 1989, p.8.

44.   Peter Baume, quoted in 'Holocaust Not Just History', *AJN*, 9 May 1986, p.8.

45.   Sam Wolski, quoted in 'Deputies Criticise Holocaust Speakers', *AJN*, 16 May 1986, p.8; 'Stop world-wide genocide – Baume', *AJT*, 8 May 1986, p.3.

46.   There are however, indications that the traditionally parochial orientation of Holocaust commemorations in Australia, focusing almost exclusively on the Jewish lessons of the Holocaust, are gradually changing. Expressions of a more outward-looking understanding of the Holocaust and its significance have begun to emerge, especially since survivors and their children and grandchildren have had a more active role in the memorial evenings. However, this increase is relative, still only a tiny fraction of commemorations, if at all, is devoted to remembering non-Jewish victims of Nazism or of other genocides; to linking aspects of the Holocaust to national contexts; or to transmitting the universal humanistic lessons of the Holocaust.

47.   B. Gillis, quoted in Press release of 1962 Warsaw Ghetto Uprising commemoration, BOD, ACC/3121/C8/2/31. The World Jewish Congress, founded in 1936 in Geneva, includes representatives of Jewish umbrella organizations from different countries.

48.   Reginald Freeson, quoted in 'Arson leniency attacked at ghetto rally', *JC*, 22 April 1966, pp.1, 12. Similarly, in 1967 he asserted: 'When a fascist thug hits a coloured man, he hits a Jew': '2,000 join in Ghetto pilgrimage', *JC*, 12 May 1967, p.11. Also, throughout the 1960s, Jewish and non-Jewish speakers explicitly condemned the British government's failure to enact suitable legislation to outlaw incitement to racial hatred.

49.   'Warsaw heroism remembered', *JC*, 25 April 1980, p.40.

50.   The commemoration was supported by other Jewish communities in New Zealand and overseas, the National Council of Churches, and the Mayors of New Zealand's four main centres and Television New Zealand's Credo production team.

51.   'New Zealand Holocaust Commemoration', *NZJC*, March 1985, p.1.

52.   The sculptor, Bob Gibb, was not Jewish.

53.   One rare exception was Wellington's 1962 memorial evening where Rabbi Gottschall asserted that the Eichmann trial represented the trial of crimes committed against humanity. 'The punishment of Eichmann is not the most important thing; it is more important that such crimes be prevented in the future against whatever nation or people they are directed': 'Warsaw Ghetto and Martyrs' Memorial Service', *NZJC*, 28 May 1962, p.7. A more recent exception was Wellington's 2003 commemoration at which George Pressburg spoke on behalf of the Allied soldiers who fought against Nazism; 'Remembering the six million', *NZJC*, June 2002, p.15.

54.   See Rabbi Lord Immanuel Jakobovitz, 'Faith, Ethics and the Holocaust: Some Personal, Theological and Religious Responses to the Holocaust', *Holocaust and Genocide Studies*, 3, 4 (1988), p.379.

55.   Jewish tradition commands that the events of the past be recalled and remembered 'as if' they happened to you personally.

56. Henry Shaw, quoted in 'No answer to "why?"', *AJN*, 8 May 1970, p.3.

57. 'Forgive and forget?', *JC*, 13 April 1977, p.12.

58. The permanent displays are based on photographs and text, supported by artefacts, documents, and artistic representations of the Holocaust, most of the latter created by survivors.

59. 'Non Jewish Victims', Jewish Holocaust Museum and Research Centre, Melbourne. The Melbourne Centre's figures seem rather low here. According to Bosworth, thirty to fifty million people died in Europe alone during the Second World War, while millions more died in Asia where there is less consensus over casualty figures; see Richard Bosworth, *Explaining Auschwitz and Hiroshima* (London: Routledge, 1994), p.9.

60. 'What was the Holocaust?', *Sydney Jewish Museum Catalogue*, 1993, p.46. 'What was the Holocaust?' specifies other groups who were maltreated, enslaved or exterminated because they had no place in the German 'People's Community'; 'Transportation to the Camps' covers the euthanasia programme and the killing of 70,000 mentally and physically disabled people; and 'Death Camps' provides estimates of all death camps victims, Jew and non-Jew alike. A sub-section on Auschwitz points out that an estimated 1,600,000 people were murdered there, including 16,000 Soviet prisoners of war, 2,000 Gypsies, and several hundred Polish political prisoners. Yet the very inclusion of these figures next to the 1,500,000 Jewish men, women and children highlights the magnitude of Jewish suffering.

61. 'Guidelines For Tour Through The Visual Display Area' (rev. edn), Holocaust Institute of WA, 1 Sept. 1993, p.4.

62. Ibid. The terms 'Death camps' and 'Extermination camps' are used interchangeably.

63. Although not stated at the time, this move was an attempt to attract more non-Jewish visitors, who would contribute to making the museum economically viable, see David Dinte, quoted in 'Sydney Jewish Museum cuts back', *AJN (Syd.)*, 10 May 1996, p.4.

64. See Shoshana Lenthen, 'Museum name change plan angers guides', *AJN (Syd.)*, 8 Dec. 1995, pp.3, 6; 'The Sydney museum', *AJN (Syd.)*, 15 Dec. 1995, p.12. See also letters on the same page from Sydney Levine and Ella Geyer.

65. Sylvia Rosenblum, quoted in Sylvia Deutsch, 'The Holocaust is unique', AJN (Melb.), 23 July 1993, p.10.

66. Justin Zimmet, 'Jonathan Morris – New Executive Director of Holocaust Centre', *Centre News*, 21, 1 (April 2002), p.7.

67. 'Multicultural Award', *Centre News*, 22, 1 (April 2003), p.3

68. 'Centre Receives Government Multiculturalism Award', *Centre News*, 21, 3 (Dec. 2002), p.8.

69. Dr Susanne Wright, 'Evaluating school visits at the Jewish Holocaust Centre', *Centre News*, 20, 3 (Dec. 2001), pp.2–3; Wright is a research fellow in the School of Education, University of Melbourne.

70. Ibid. This was in response to the question 'What will you remember most from your visit?'.

71. Ibid.

72. Justice Marcus Einfeld, 'Our Generation's Responsibility', *Centre News*, 22, 1 (April 2003), p.24.

73. Sophie Gelski, *Teaching the Holocaust* (Sydney: Sydney Jewish Museum, 2003).

74. 'Teaching our Children', *Sydney Jewish Museum Newsletter*, Spring 2003, p.3.

75. These stories can either be read or heard through handsets.

76. 'Holocaust Memories', *NZJC*, Dec./Jan. 1997/8, p.13.

77. Other aspects of the three-hour visit include an Israel experience, including food tasting and Israeli dancing, and a tour of the synagogue together with explanations about Jewish festivals, traditions and religious practices.

78. Hanka Pressburg paraphrased in 'Hanka Pressburg', *NZJC*, March 1995, p.7.
79. Hanka Pressburg, personal communication, Dec. 2001.
80. High-profile temporary Holocaust exhibitions in Britain have included the 1961 Warsaw Ghetto Uprising exhibition in the East End of London, the 1983 Auschwitz exhibition and various travelling Anne Frank exhibitions.
81. Leon Greenman, *Auschwitz Survivor 98288: A Resource for Holocaust Education* (London: Jewish Museum, 1996).
82. Quoted in ibid.
83. In this way the IWM's conceptual approach to other victims of Nazism is similar to that of the US Holocaust Memorial Museum.
84. Stephen Smith, personal communication, 6 July 2003.
85. Beth Shalom provides visitors with a more detailed history of anti-Semitism in Britain and Europe than Holocaust museums established by Jewish people. This is probably because Jews have been more careful not to offend the predominantly non-Jewish audiences.
86. Beth Shalom Holocaust exhibition; see also Stephen D. Smith, *Making Memory: Creating Britain's First Holocaust Centre* (Newark, UK: Quill, 2002), p.154.
87. The £17 million new wing was funded mainly through a £12.6 million grant from the National Lottery Fund along with major pledges.

CHAPTER 4

1. '"Concentration camp holiday" book storm', *JC*, 10 April 1981, p.48.
2. Cited in 'Verbal abuse', *AJN (Melb.)*, 26 Dec. 1997, p.2.
3. Dr M.L.M. Wall, letter to editor, *NZJC*, April 1981, p.2.
4. Ibid.
5. For a more detailed discussion about the evolution of the use of the term Holocaust, see Leon A. Jick, 'The Holocaust: Its Use and Abuse within the American Public', *Yad Vashem Studies*, XIV (1981), pp.303-18.
6. See Benjamin Wilkomirski, *Fragments* (London: Picador, 1997); Donald Watt, *Stoker: The Story of an Australian Who Survived Auschwitz-Berkenau* (Sydney: Simon & Schuster, 1995); Helen Demidenko reinvented herself as a relation of victims of alleged Judeobolshevism: *The Hand That Signed The Paper* (Sydney: Allen & Unwin, 1994).
7. Saba Feniger, quoted in Victor Kleerekoper, 'Refugees, traumas but no Holocaust', *AJN (Melb.)*, 16 Nov. 2001, p.6.
8. Stephen Levine, *The New Zealand Jewish Community* (New York: Lexington Books, 1999), p.108.
9. Peter Novick, *The Holocaust in American Life* (New York: Houghton Mifflin, 1999), p.242.
10. Ibid., pp.243–4.
11. Chantal Abitbol, 'A question of numbers', *AJN (Melb.)*, 1 Feb. 2002, p.17; Danya Levy, 'Nazi camp comparisons "unacceptable": Ruddock', *AJN (Melb.)*, 15 Feb. 2002, p.3.
12. Philip Adams, 'Help turn the tide of lies – Your support counts!', *Australian*, 23 Feb. 2002.
13. Stan Marks, 'Woomera inmates', letter, *AJN (Melb.)*, 19 April 2002, p.32. This is not a case of suffering that falls short of the benchmark of one's own experiences being cruelly relativised. Many of those who spoke out against such analogies, in many cases Holocaust survivors and their descendants, are extremely sympathetic to the plight of asylum seekers. They have been most vocal in expressing their

condemnation of the government's refugee policy and the internment and treatment of refugees in detention centres.

14. Philip Adams, 'Welcome to our gulags', *Australian*, 6 April 2002.

15. Michael Leunig, cited in 'Cruel absurdities?', letter to the editor, *AJN (Melb.)*, 7 June 2002, p.17.

16. Alana Rosenbaum, 'Leunig's "inappropriate" cartoon rejected by *The Age*', *AJN (Melb.)*, 17 May 2002, p.3.

17. Indeed, Leunig's cartoon appears in the midst of a spate of political cartoons in Australia which Professsor Andrew Markus has found to overwhelmingly demonstrate an anti-Israel imbalance in their interpretation of the Middle East conflict; Andrew Markus, 'Political cartoonists and the ME conflict', *AJN (Melb.)*, 27 Sept. 2002, p.18.

18. An Alan Moir cartoon, which in effect equated the Warsaw Ghetto of 1943 with the West Bank of 2003, echoed Leunig's cartoon; see *Sydney Morning Herald*, 12 Aug. 2003. For Australian Jewish responses to this cartoon see, 'Cartoonists must draw a line', *AJN (Melb.)*, 22 Aug. 2003, p.14; Ruth Wajnryb, 'Deconstructing Alan Moir's offensive cartoon', *AJN (Melb.)*, 29 Aug. 2003, p.16.

19. Howard Jacobson, 'Wordsmiths and Atrocities against Language: The Incendiary use of the Holocaust and Nazism against Jews', and also Winston Pickett, 'Nasty or Nazi? The use of Antimsemitic Topoi by the Left-liberal Media', in Paul Iganski and Barry Kosmin (eds.), *A New Antisemitism?: Debating Judeophobia in 21st Century Britain* (London: Profile, 2003), pp.102–13, 148–69. With regards to New Zealand, see 'Are these cartoons anti-Semitic?', *NZJC*, May 2002, p.5; Henry Benjamin and Mike Regan, 'New Zealand cartoonist fired', *AJN (Melb.)*, 22 Aug. 2003, p.3; Mike Regan, 'Israel and Jews cited in Herald cartoonist's sacking', *NZJC*, Sept. 2003, p.3.

20. Matthew E. Berger, 'How different is the "road map"?', *AJN (Melb.)*, 9 May 2003, p.10.

21. For more about *Yom haShoah* commemorations in Australia see Judith E. Berman, *Holocaust Remembrance in Australian Jewish Communities, 1945–2000* (Perth: University of Western Australia Press, 2001).

22. Also, the survivors who were involved in the establishment of many of the museums did not necessarily share this ideological perspective.

23. Ben Korman, personal communication, 8 Jan. 1997; also Jenny Wajsenberg, July 1991 seminar with Holocaust Institute of WA guides and survivors; Holocaust Institute of WA archives (audio tape).

24. For more about the trauma of post-Holocaust world Jewry see Yehuda Bauer, 'We are condemned to remember', *Jerusalem Post*, 19 April, 2001. This chapter has limited itself to examining whether the Holocaust has been misused to convey the Zionist lesson of the Holocaust at *Yom haShoah* commemorations. An examination of 'March of the Living', which has been criticized for exploiting the Holocaust both to increase Jewish identity and unity as well as to boost Zionist support, is largely beyond the confines of this book, although the subject is touched upon in a different context in Chapter Five.

25. James E. Young, *The Texture of Memory: Holocaust Memorials and Meaning* (New Haven, CT: Yale University Press, 1993), pp.209–17.

26. Dr J. Schneeweiss, quoted in 'Youth Leader Claims Neglect', *Australian Jewish Times* (hereafter *AJT*), 11 May 1978, p.3. See also Howard Cooper and Paul Morrison, *A Sense of Belonging* (London: Weidenfeld & Nicolson, 1991), pp.114–15.

27. Bill Rubinstein, letter to the editor, *AJN (Melb.)*, 4 April 2003, p.17. No figures exist for the intermarriage rate in New Zealand but anecdotal evidence suggests at least the same rate as Australia and probably higher; Steven Sedley, personal communication, 11 Nov. 2002.

28. 'Warsaw Jewish Heroes Remembered', *JC*, 17 April 1953, p.5.
29. For example, see 'Auckland Jewry Remembers', *NZJC*, 20 May 1963, p.7.
30. Rabbi Astor, quoted in 'Warsaw Ghetto and "Martyrs" Memorial Service', *NZJC* 28 May 1962, p.7. See also, Marcus Einfeld, quoted in 'Memorial Day in Sydney calls for "Remembering Martyrs and Work for Future"', *AJT*, 21 April 1977, p.5.
31. Rabbi Lubofsky, quoted in 'Ghetto Memorial', *SJN*, 3 May 1968, p.2.
32. Ibid.
33. David Berinson, quoted in 'Yom Ha Shoa', *Maccabean*, 4 May 1990, p.3.
34. Joshua Henzel, 'The Diaspora's "Quiet Holocaust"', *AJN (Melb.)*, 15 Jan. 1999, p.2. Rev. Dan Levy, the minister for Enfield and Winchmore Hill in Britain, was also worried about soaring assimilation rates when he advocated that monies for Holocaust projects be redirected towards the provision of affordable full-time Jewish education to prevent, what he described as, 'the self-inflicted Holocaust' of 'Jewish ignorance'; James Kaye, 'Centre slammed', *London Jewish News*, 16 June 2000, p.3.
35. Jack Kronhill, 'The Quiet Holocaust', 'Letters', *AJN* (Melb.), 22 Jan. 1999, p.25.
36. Ibid.
37. Eli Sat, quoted in 'Habo man to counter Jewish decline here', *AJT*, 1 Nov. 1984, p.26. Habonim is a Zionist youth movement.
38. Dr Wolf Matsdorf, 'Abuse of Holocaust', 'Letters', *AJT*, 13 Dec. 1984, p.6.
39. Evelyn Wilcock, 'Holocaust and mixed marriages', Letter to the editor, *JC*, 24 April 1992, p.14.
40. *AJR Review*, xxvii, 7 (July 1972), p.5.
41. For more about international debates about the connection between the Holocaust and Jewish identity, see Jonathan Webber (ed.), *Jewish Identities in the New Europe* (London: Littman Library of Jewish Civilization, 1994).
42. British Chief Rabbi Sir Jonathan Sacks, quoted in Chaim Bermant, 'Is it not time to tone down the mourning?', *AJN (Melb.)*, 6 Aug. 1993, p.18. See also, Robert Alter, 'Deformations of the Holocaust', *Commentary*, 71, 2 (Feb. 1981), p.51.
43. Clive Lawton, personal communication, 8 July 2003; Dr Steven Zipperstein, cited in David Winner, 'Don't let Holocaust dominate our lives', *JC*, 3 April 1987, p.10.
44. 'Mill Hill minister slams "Holocaust obsession"', *JC*, 9 April 1999, p.9.
45. David Bryfman, 'How do we commemorate the Shoah without survivors?', *Zachor: Journal of the Australian Association of Jewish Holocaust Survivors and Descendants* (Sept. 2002), p.8.
46. *Collins Concise Dictionary*, Australian edition (London: Collins, 1989).
47. Ibid.
48. 'Memorial to Martyrs', *JC*, 18 May 1979, p.6.
49. Rabbi Astor, paraphrased in 'Warsaw Ghetto and Martyrs' Memorial Service', *NZJC*, 28 May 1962, p.7.
50. The Nuremberg Laws determined that not only those who identified as Jews were classified as such but also those who had converted from Judaism to Christianity. This inaccurate use of 'martyrs' obfuscates the crucial distinction between traditional Christian anti-Semitism and Nazi racist anti-Semitism which was based on 'blood' and 'racial origin' which were permanent and therefore made change or coexistence impossible.
51. Dayan M. Steinberg, cited in 'Remembering The 6,000,000 Martyrs', *JC*, 13 April 1956, p.9; see also Rabbi Rubin-Zacks, cited in 'Battle of the Warsaw Ghetto Anniversary', *Westralian Judean*, May 1945, p.7; 'Warsaw Ghetto Commemoration', *Maccabean Bulletin*, May 1945, pp.17–18.
52. Cyla Sokolowicz, Editorial, *Centre News*, 1, 4 (Dec. 1985), p.3. This is just one example among many such uses by contributors to *Centre News*.
53. The *Bund* was a political organization, based on the model of the Jewish socialist

party in Eastern and Central Europe, which upheld the viability of Jewish cultural identity in a social democratic Europe through which *Yiddish* secular culture could flourish.

54. Literally translated as a 'Memorial and a Name'.

55. Interestingly, references to the 'martyrs' of the Holocaust having died '*al kiddush Hashem*' are almost non-existent in Holocaust museums where Jewish victims of Nazism are more commonly referred to as 'the six million, "murdered victims"' and the Warsaw Ghetto fighters as 'fallen heroes'. This different use in terminology is explained by the perception that use of unemotive language is the most effective and appropriate means of narrating the story of the Holocaust in educational institutions.

CHAPTER 5

1. David Thelen, 'Introduction: Memory and American History', in David Thelen (ed.), *Memory and American History* (Bloomington, IN: Indiana University Press, 1989), p.xvi.

2. Paula Hamilton, 'The Knife Edge: Debates About Memory and History', in Kate Darian-Smith and Paula Hamilton (eds.), *Memory and History in Twentieth-Century Australia* (London: Oxford University Press, 1994), p.15.

3. John R. Gillis, 'Memory and Identity: The History of a Relationship', in John R. Gillis (ed.), *Commemorations: the Politics of National Identity* (New Jersey: Princeton University Press, 1994), p.3.

4. Peter Novick, *The Holocaust in American Life* (New York: Houghton Mifflin, 1999).

5. James E. Young, *The Texture of Memory: Holocaust Memorials and Meaning* (New Haven, CT: Yale University Press, 1993), p.263.

6. Lucette Valensi, 'From Sacred History to Historical Memory and Back: The Jewish Past', *History and Anthropology*, 2 (1986), p.286. See also Young, *Texture of Memory*, pp.209–10.

7. Yosef Hayim Yerushalmi, *Zakhor: Jewish History and Jewish Memory*, 2nd edn (New York: Schocken Books, 1989), p.9. Zakhor is the Hebrew word for 'remember'. Yerushalmi's book *Zakhor*, which explores the channels that sustained Jewish historical memory, documents the emergence of a Jewish historiographical tradition and the erosion of Jewish historical memory in the nineteenth century.

8. For example, '"Commemorate Warsaw Ghetto with Cultural Projects" Says W.J.C.', *AJN (Melb.)*, 15 April 1955, p.2.

9. *El Mole Rachamim* is the Hebrew memorial prayer for the dead that asks God to take the soul of the departed into his keeping. The prayer is chanted at funerals and unveilings, visits to the cemetery, in the synagogues before *yahrzeits* (anniversary of a death) and at *yiskor* (memorials). *Kadish*, the mourner's prayer, that praises the greatness of God, is traditionally recited in public by someone in mourning. A *yahrzeit* candle is traditionally lit on the anniversary of a death.

10. The Jewish Lads' Brigade is actively involved in Britain and New Zealand. The beginning of the ceremony is marked with the slow tapping of drums while the multicoloured standard bearers from branches of AJEX march through the hall onto the platform, dipping their banners as the whole audience rises in silent remembrance. To mark the end of the commemoration, the Jewish Lads' Brigade buglers sound The Last Post and Reveille, and the audience stands to sing the national anthem and the *Hatikvah*.

11. Reform, Progressive and Liberal strands of Judaism have much in common. Reform Judaism, a modern religious movement which has its roots in Germany in

the early nineteenth century, broke away from some aspects of traditional Jewish law and practice. In Australia about 15–20 per cent of Jews are Progressive. A history of the Progressive movement in Australia and an account of its strained relations with Orthodox Jewry is provided by W. D. Rubinstein, *The Jews in Australia: A Thematic History* (Melbourne: William Heinemann, 1991), II, pp.184–200. In 1990, about 24 per cent of households with synagogue memberships in Britain belonged to Reform or Liberal synagogues; W. D. Rubinstein, A History of the *Jews in the English-Speaking World: Great Britain* (London: Macmillan, 1996), p.409. In the mid 1990s, New Zealand's Orthodox congregations had about twice as many members as the Liberals: Anne Beaglehole and Hal Levine, *Far From the Promised Land: Being Jewish in New Zealand* (Wellington: Pacific Press, 1995), p.65.

12. Beaglehole and Levine, *Far From the Promised Land*, p.65.
13. Liberal Temples were formed in Auckland in 1950 and Wellington in 1960. Other major areas of conflict have been over conversion, catering for the children of the intermarried, and burial rights.
14. The situation in Wellington is further complicated as the community centre is located by the Orthodox synagogue but facilities are shared by the two congregations.
15. 'Departing rabbi stresses cooperation', *NZJC*, Sept. 2001, pp.16–17.
16. Moreover, students from Moriah School, the only Jewish school in Wellington, were not allowed to attend a Reform synagogue in an official capacity and therefore could not perform as a group (such as in a dramatic production or a choir).
17. Anonymous, personal communication, Dec. 2001.
18. Anonymous, personal communication, Dec. 2001.
19. Anonymous, personal communication, Dec. 2001.
20. Anonymous, personal communication, 19 Feb. 2002.
21. Anonymous, personal communication, Dec. 2001. In Auckland the Reform and Orthodox communities have generally held separate Holocaust commemorations. A joint commemoration in 2002 produced the following comment: 'But for me one of the very special aspects was the coming together of members of both Orthodox and Progressive congregations under one roof to commemorate the event together. May it be the forerunner of many more similar occasions. That is also how it should be in our small community.' Wally Hirsh, 'An Auckland view', *NZJC*, May 2002, p.21.
22. This arrangement was not always enough to deter antagonisms. Although Manchester's 1971 *Yom haShoah* commemoration was held in the King David School hall, two Orthodox ministers walked out when the minister of Manchester's Reform synagogue introduced the guest speaker; 'Ministers walk out at ghetto service', *JC*, 30 April 1971, p.36.
23. 'Liberal protest over Martyrs' Memorial', *AJT*, 23 April 1970, p.1. This was the second time that controversy surrounded the monument. The first was when members of the Yiddish-speaking community protested that a Yiddish inscription was not being included in the memorial plaque. The monument's organizers eventually agreed since most the six million, in whose memory the monument was being erected, considered Yiddish as their mother-tongue.
24. 'Board Moves On Memorial Split', *SJN*, 1 May 1970, p.3.
25. 'Concern expressed over memorial issue', *AJT*, 30 April 1970, p.7. *Chevra Kadisha* are Jewish funeral societies which provide services related to Jewish funerals, burials and mourning.
26. 'Consecration without Liberals', *SJN*, 8 May 1970, p.3.
27. In 1978 most Orthodox Rabbis in Sydney had boycotted the annual Martyrs' Memorial Service at Rookwood cemetery (which complements the main commemoration): 'Reverence To Our Martyrs', *AJT*, 18 May 1978, p.2; 'UOS

Protest Prayer Of "Breakaways" At Martyrs' Memorial', *AJT*, 1 June 1978, p.2; 'Board "Dismay" At UOS Statements', *AJT*, 8 June 1978, p.3. In 1980 Orthodox Rabbis again refused to attend the Rookwood commemoration, and the Federation of Orthodox Jewish Synagogues held a separate martyrs memorial observance, because Temple Emanuel's Rev Michael Deutsch had been asked to conduct the Rookwood service, and Temple Emanuel Woollahra's chief minister, Rabbi Brian Fox, had been chosen as one of the main speakers. 'Separate Martyrs' Ceremony', *AJT*, 10 April 1980, p.1; 'Record crowd at cemetery service', *AJT*, 17 April 1980, p.3; 'Av Beth Din Wants No Secular Memorials', ibid.; 'Committee To Plan Martyrs' Memorial', *AJT*, 8 Jan. 1981, p.17.

28. *Annual Report of the New South Wales Jewish Board of Deputies, 1981*, p.8.

29. Leslie Caplan, quoted in 'Deputies told: "do your duty"', *AJT*, 6 May 1982, pp.3, 20.

30. 'Needless confrontation', *AJN (Syd.)*, 15 April 1994, p.18. Many of the Orthodox rabbinate attended the Martyrs Memorial Service at Rookwood cemetery in 1994, but not the main community one. *AJN (Melb.)*, 7 Nov. 1997, p.5.

31. Rabbi Selwyn Franklin, quoted in 'Yom haShoah commemorations – The Orthodox View', *AJN (Syd.)*, 15 April 1994, p.18.

32. Sophie Caplan, personal communication, 7 Feb. 1996. A sermon about the Holocaust and special prayers to the 'martyrs' are included in regular services at Orthodox synagogues but no combined Orthodox commemoration has taken place since 1983 when Rabbi Silberman and some other affiliates of the NSW Association of Orthodox Jewish Ministers organized a separate, more religious *Yom haShoah* service for their congregations, in the Bondi Mizrachi Synagogue. The Liberal community continues to attend commemoration services at the Liberal synagogue and some Liberal Rabbis and members also attend the main community function.

33. Rabbi Shalom Coleman, personal communication, 30 Aug. 1995. At the 1973 commemoration Jack Krasnostein, President of the Board of Deputies, pointed out that it was a lay gathering and that religious services were held by the Perth Hebrew Congregation and at Temple David. See 'Perth's Jewry Honours the Heroes of the Warsaw Ghetto', *Maccabean*, 4 May 1973, p.1.

34. Avraham Zeleznikow, personal communication, 20 Nov. 1995. Sophie Caplan has suggested that this problem may not have arisen in Melbourne because no Liberal clergy member in that community was a Holocaust survivor, not because of greater tolerance in that Jewish community.

35. From 1983, commemorations at the Holocaust monument in Hyde Park complemented the indoor commemorations, organised by the PJEX.

36. National Yad Vashem Charitable Trust minutes, 7 March 1986, Appendix I, ACC/3121/C23/1/2, BDA.

37. Editorial, 'Remembering', *JC*, 28 March 1986, p.22.

38. YVCUK minutes, 27 Oct. 1986, ACC/3121/C23/1/2, BDA.

39. F. Barschak, 'Poor turnout at memorial', letter to editor, *JC*, 16 May 1986, p.22; Brigit Grant, 'Celebration of survival', *JC*, 9 May 1986, p.6.

40. Barschak, 'Poor turnout'.

41. YVCUK minutes, 21 May 1987, ACC/3121C23/01/01, BDA.

42. Ben Helfgott, quoted in David Winner, 'Holocaust Memorial desecrated', *JC*, 1 May 1987, p.10.

43. National Yad Vashem Charitable Trust minutes, 24 Oct. 1989, ACC/3121/C23/1/2, BDA.

44. David Winner, 'Candles and tears at Hyde Park', *JC*, 5 May 1989, p.8.

45. YVCUK minutes, 12 March 1992, BDA.

46. Sam Pivnick, cited in Caroline Bass, 'Young and old commemorate the victims of

the Holocaust', *JC*, 1 May 1992, p.8.

47.   For example, see Irene Daniels, 'Unworthy', *JC*, 5 Aug. 1983, p.14; Kitty Hart-Moxon, 'Board's record on Holocaust centre', letter to the editor, *JC*, 29 Sept. 1995, p.24.

48.   Freda Wineman, 'A survivor excluded', letter to editor, *JC*, 8 July 1983, p.16.

49.   Board of Deputies of British Jews, Annual Report 1997, BDA. See also Henry D. Myer, letter to the editor, *JC*, 15 July 1983.

50.   'A time to remember', editorial, *JC*, 16 April 1993, p.12. Acknowledging its failure to attract significant attendance, the YVCUK decided, after much deliberation, to combine the 1997 *Yom haShoah* commemoration at the Dell with the annual indoor Warsaw Ghetto Uprising memorial meeting. This change had little impact on attendance trends – there were few youth at the 1998 and 1999 commemorations and the Board was still not very supportive in insisting that *Yom haShoah* be commemorated. Ben Helfgott, cited in YVCUK minutes, 20 May 1998, BDA.

51.   Cheadle Hulme and Eva E. Gillalt, 'Holocaust Memorial Day', letters, *Association of Jewish Refugees Information (AJR Information)*, LIV, 12 (1999), p.6.

52.   Susan Pollack, quoted in Jon Fenton-Fischer, 'A day to mourn the murdered', *Hendon and Finchley Press*, 11 Jan. 2001, p.22.

53.   'Board Welcomes Home Office Consultation Paper', Board of Deputies Press Release, 18 Oct. 1999, www.bod.org.uk, accessed 29/07/00.

54.   Rabbi Lord Immanuel Jakobovitz, 'Faith, ethics and the Holocaust: Some personal, theological and religious responses to the Holocaust', *Holocaust and Genocide Studies*, 3, 4 (1988), p.372.

55.   Douglas Davis, 'UK Holocaust commemoration', *Jerusalem Post Internet Edition*, 17 Jan. 2000, www.jpost.com, accessed 17/01/00.

56.   Jonathan Sacks quoted in Philip Johnston, 'Holocaust day "to let Britons reflect on evil in the world"', *Electronic Telegraph*, issue 1707, 27 Jan. 2000, www.telegraph.co.uk, accessed 27/01/00.

57.   Rabbi Tony Bayfield quoted in Philip Johnston, 'Date of liberation of Auschwitz is day to remember Holocaust', *Electronic Telegraph*, issue 1607, 19 Oct. 1999, www.telegraph.co.uk, accessed 27/01/00.

58.   A variety of individuals and political groups voiced their opposition to Holocaust Memorial Day. Those cited in the following paragraphs represent the range of issues raised.

59.   Gerda Mayer, *AJR Information*, LV, 3 (2000), p.6.

60.   Margaret Grundmann, 'Holocaust Memorial Day', Letters, *AJR Information*, LIV, 10 (1999), p.7.

61.   'Holocaust Day', letter to editor, *JC*, 26 Jan. 2001, p.28.

62.   Dan Stone, 'Day of Remembrance or Day of Forgetting: Or, Why Britain Does Not Need a Holocaust Memorial Day', *Patterns of Prejudice*, 34, 4 (2000), p.50.

63.   Ibid., pp.50–1.

64.   Frank Bright, 'UK Holocaust Remembrance Day', letters to the editor, *AJR Information*, LV, 2 (2000), p.6. 'Britain and the Holocaust', the theme of the second Holocaust Memorial Day, was the focus of heated debates between two leading Jewish historians in Britain, see David Cesarani, 'Grate Britain?', *JC*, 25 Jan. 2002, p.34; Bill Rubinstein, 'No blame attaches to this country', *JC*, 8 Feb. 2002, p.25.

65.   Norman Lebrecht, 'Don't consign the dead to an empty day', *JC*, 2000.

66.   Simon Sebag-Montefiore, 'Holocaust Day must speak for all victims', *Evening Standard*, 23 Jan. 2001, p.13. See also, 'The Holocaust remembered', Editorial, *Daily Telegraph*, 27 Jan. 2001, p.25.

67.   Ed Kessler, quoted in Davis, 'UK Holocaust commemoration'.

68.   Johnston, 'Date of liberation'.

69.   Douglas Davis, 'UK Holocaust commemoration', Jerusalem Post Internet Edition,

17 Jan. 2000, www.jpost.com, accessed 17/01/00.

70. Ronnie Landau, 'Holocaust Day: the Legacy', *JC*, 26 Jan. 2001, pp.30–1.

71. Norman Lebrecht, 'Who's in command at the command performance?', *JC*, 2 March 2001, p.33; Gaby Koppel, 'Shoah events seats', Letter, *JC*, 23 March 2001, p.31; Jo Wagerman, 'Holocaust Day seating plans', *JC*, 13 April 2001, p.25.

72. Jo Wagerman, 'Holocaust Day seating plans', *JC*, 13 April 2001, p.25.

73. Geoffrey Alderman, 'Disband this body of (un)representatives', *JC*, 1 March 2002, p.27.

74. Cyla Sokolowicz, 'Editorial', *Centre News*, 6, 4 (Dec. 1989), p.3.

75. Jack Kugelmass, 'The Rites of the Tribe: The Meaning of Poland for American Jewish Tourists' in Jack Kugelmass (ed.), *Going Home*, YIVO Annual 21 (Evanston, IL: North Western Press, 1993), p.402.

76. Simon Frisner, 'Warsaw visit', letter to editor, *JC*, 18 March 1983, p.20.

77. M. Scherer, 'Don't go to Warsaw', letter to the editor, *JC*, 7 Jan. 1983, p.19.

78. In fact, two annual communal functions in commemoration of the Holocaust did take place in London over a decade but this was not due to the conflict between the Board and the PJEX but rather a result of the establishment of Britain's first permanent Holocaust memorial in public space, the Holocaust Memorial Garden at The Dell in Hyde Park.

79. Julian Robinson, 'Deputies delegation to visit Poland', *JC*, 24 Dec. 1982, p.4. The PJEX's stance would not have been a minority opinion in Australia where the Executive Council of Australian Jewry voted to oppose official representation of the community.

80. Julian Robinson, Zeev Ben-Shlomo and Yoram Kessel, 'Warsaw visit attacked', *JC*, 15 April 1983, p.1.

81. Gabriel Rey, 'Pilgrimage to Poland', *JC*, 6 May 1983, p.20.

82. Reference was made to the letter in question, dated 15th April, in PJEX to the President of the Board of Deputies; 20 May 1983, ACC 3121/E4/763, BDA.

83. Correspondence to Hayim Pinner (secretary of the Board of Deputies), 28 July 1983, ACC 3121/E4/763, BDA.

84. Referred to in PJEX to the President of the Board of Deputies, 20 May 1983, ACC 3121/E4/763, BDA.

85. Ibid.

86. PJEX to the President of the Board of Deputies, 20 May 1983, ACC 3121/E4/763, BDA.

87. The sources refer to the Warsaw Ghetto Memorial organizing committee and the Holocaust Memorial Meeting organizing committee interchangeably.

88. Greville Janner to Simon Frisner, 11 Aug. 1983, ACC 3121/E4/763, BDA.

89. Board of Deputies memo, 20 Oct. 1983. ACC3121/E4/763, BDA. Ironically, ten years later the Board, following lead from the World Jewish Congress, considered boycotting the annual commemorations in Warsaw when it appeared that the nuns at the controversially established Carmelite convent would not be moving to their new site.

90. Yael Zerubavel, *Recovered Roots: Collective Memory and the Making of Israeli National Tradition* (Chicago: University of Chicago Press, 1995), p.xix.

91. Cited in Walt Secord, 'Community divided on tours to Poland', *AJN*, 11 Aug. 1989, p.5.

92. Victor Kleerekoper, 'Melbourne Jewry votes against Poland tours', *AJT*, 6 Oct. 1989, p.25.

93. Cited in 'Sydney leaders express support for organized tours', *AJT*, 22 Sept., 1989, p.15.

94. Secord, 'Community divided on tours to Poland'.

95. Cited in 'Sydney leaders express support for organized tours'.

96. Michael Gawenda, 'March of the Living an unseemly extravaganza', *AJT*, 22 Sept. 1989, p.15.
97. Secord, 'Community divided on tours to Poland'.
98. 'March of the living in the country of the dead', *AJT*, 28 July 1989, p.5.
99. Cited in 'Sydney leaders express support for organized tours'.
100. Ibid.
101. Dr Mark Spigelman, letters to editor, *AJT*, 18 Aug. 1989, p.12.
102. A Moriah College student, Australia's sole representative on the first MOTL in 1988, was the exception.
103. For examples, see 'On the record', *AJN*, 18 May 2001, p.22.
104. Of course, there were still those who had their doubts. For example, Dr George Foster, President of the AAJHS&D, explained that survivors were worried about stories of Jewish youth from other countries attending nightclubs in Warsaw or having wild drinking parties in their hotels; Samantha Baden, 'Shoah survivors split over March of the Living', *AJN*, 6 April 2001, p.3. However, by 2003 the Association had become a patron of the March and participates in a Consultative Committee; Dr George Foster, President's Report, *Zachor*, Sept. 2003, p.3.
105. Baden, 'Shoah survivors split'.
106. David J. Forman, 'The Mockery of the March', *AJN*, 22 March 2002, p.17.
107. Bianca Jonovic, 'Why the March must go to Israel', *AJN (Melb.)*, 29 March 2002, p.17.
108. Brandon Cohen, 'Australia cancels "March" to Israel', *AJN*, 5 April 2002, p.3. After much discussion, Australian organizers had decided to let participants choose – to spend *Yom ha'Atzmaut* in Israel as part of a United Israel Appeal solidarity mission, or to spend it in London with British and American students.

CHAPTER 6

1. Saul Friedlander, 'The *Shoah* Between Memory and History', *Jerusalem Quarterly*, 53 (Winter 1990), p.126.
2. W. D. Rubinstein, *The Jews in Australia: A Thematic History* (Melbourne: William Heinemann, 1991), II, p.6. An exception to this non-universalistic trend, according to Philip Mendes, was the active and vociferous involvement of left-wing Jewish students in the anti-Vietnam war movement. However, he acknowledges that although individual students and a few organizations were active in the campaign, the Jewish leadership and the mainstream Jewish organizations remained silent on the issue; Philip Mendes, *The New Left, The Jews and the Vietnam War, 1965–72* (Melbourne: Lazare, 1993), pp.131–2.
3. For a more detailed analysis see Judith E. Berman, *Holocaust Remembrance in Australian Jewish Communities, 1945–2000* (Perth: University of Western Australia Press, 2001).
4. Ibid.
5. Quoted in Michael Marrus, 'The Use and Misuse of the Holocaust', in Peter Hayes (ed.), *Lessons and Legacies: The Meaning of the Holocaust in a Changing World* (Evanston, IL: Northwestern University Press), 1991, p.116.
6. Mendes, *The New Left*, p.143.
7. The AJDS was not accepted into the Jewish Community Council of Victoria (JCCV) until 1993. The AJDS and the Sydney Jewish Left (which existed until the late 1990s) maintained an outward looking approach, concerned particularly with racial discrimination.
8. Sam Lipski, 'How parochialism made us political', *AJN (Melb.)*, 19 Nov. 1999, p.17.
9. Philip Mendes, 'Political Jews', Letters, *AJN (Melb.)*, 3 Dec. 1999, p.14.
10. I thank Bill Rubinstein for these insights, personal communication, 21 May 2002.

In 2000, Deborah Stone, editor of the *AJN* wrote 'I think as a Jewish newspaper, we have an obligation to cover racial matters, reconciliation, human rights issues, and migration and refugees – we have an obligation to these people and issues from what we, as Jews, have learnt from our past, from our own experiences of historical trauma'; Deborah Stone, 'The Holocaust and Responsibilities of a Jewish Newspaper', *Centre News*, 19, 2 (2000), p.13.

11. Philip Mendes, personal communication, 27 May 2002.

12. This research adopts a wide definition of Jewish Holocaust survivor that includes Jews who were resident in Nazi-occupied Europe for any period of time between 1933 and 1945. In this category are those who left Nazi-occupied Europe pre-war, those who survived the Holocaust in concentration camps, in death camps, in labour camps, in hiding, or who fled their homes to the Soviet Union to escape Nazism.

13. Kathy Grinblat, *Children of the Shadows* (Perth: University of Western Australia Press, 2002); Ruth Wajnryb, *The Silence: how tragedy shapes talk*, Sydney, 2001.

14. 'Leaders speak out against Hanson', *AJN (Melb.)*, 6 Dec. 1996; Bernard Freedman, 'Hanson triumph shocks Jewish community', *AJN (Melb.)*, 19 June 1998; 'Rabbis call on PM to condemn Hanson "evil"', *AJN (Melb.)*, 30 May 1997; Editorial, 'The Hanson anxiety', *AJN (Melb.)*, 2 March 2001, p.14; all accessed at http://www.ajn.com.au/pages/archives.

15. 'Racism seminar hits out at Jewish "apathy"', *AJN (Syd.)*, 15 Aug. 1997, p.7. *B'nai B'rith*'s Anti-Defamation Commission has been active since 1979, combating racism and anti-Semitism, through education programmes, media briefings, liaison with key community decision-makers, and research.

16. 'Students rally against One Nation', *AJN (Melb.)*, 3 July 1998. In December 1996 an anti-racism rally in Melbourne attracted the participation of many youth organizations; Margaret Safran, 'Jews rally in force against racism', *AJN (Melb.)*, 13 Dec. 1996. In May 1997 about 300 Sydney Jews, headed by ECAJ President Diane Shteinman, took a prominent part in an anti-racism rally; Vic Alhadeff, 'Sydney Jews say "No!" to racism', *AJN (Melb.)*, 23 May 1997; all accessed at http://www.ajn.com.au/pages/archives.

17. 'Students rally against One Nation'; For similar comments see Justice Marcus Einfeld, cited in Editorial, 'The Hanson anxiety', *AJN (Melb.)*, 2 March 2001, p.14.

18. Victor Kleerkoper, 'Education: a punishment to fit the crime', *AJN (Melb.)*, 7 Jan. 2000, p.5. The museum's president is Shmuel Rosenkranz, a pre-war refugee from Nazism. A recent flier boldly states: 'The Holocaust Museum and Research Centre is working to combat racism, and preserve the Australian tradition of tolerance and acceptance'.

19. Floris Kalman, Editorial, 'Honouring The Past – Building For The Future', *Centre News*, 17, 2 (1999), p.2.

20. 'Racism in schools', *Centre News*, 19, 3 (2000), p.18. Professor Andrew Markus, director of the Centre for Jewish Civilisation at Monash University and a child of pre-war refugees from Nazism, opened the seminar. The keynote speech was given by Basil Varghese, education coordinator for the Brotherhood of St Lawrence.

21. 'Volunteer – Lotte Weiss', *Zachor: The Australian Association of Jewish Holocaust Survivors and Descendants Journal*, Sept. 2001, p.15.

22. The Courage to Care exhibition was developed in 1992 by the Jewish Museum in Melbourne in conjunction with the Raoul Wallenberg Unit of *B'nai B'rith*, and the JHM&RC. In 1997 it was converted into a travelling exhibition and toured Victoria, New South Wales, Western Australia, South Australia and Queensland. Over 80,000 people have visited the exhibition since its inception.

23. Masha Zeleznikow, quoted in Brandon Cohen, 'Courage to Care returns triumphant', *AJN* (Melb.), 17 Aug. 2001, p.16. The Anti-Defamation Unit of *B'nai*

B'rith is currently preparing 'Fair Go Australia', an anti-racism programme to be launched in March 2003 and supported by the state governments in NSW, Victoria and Queensland. The programme uses the internet to provide victims of racism the opportunity of a confidential and anonymous platform to receive help from qualified professionals; 'Australian anti-racism programs to go abroad', *AJN (Melb.)*, 23 Aug. 2002, p.7.

24.   Shaun Jackson, representing Perth's youth, addressed the commemoration at the Holocaust monument in Supreme Court Gardens; Ron Samuel addressed the main community commemoration at the Jewish Centre.

25.   Brandon Cohen, 'Youth commemorate the shoah', *AJN (Melb.)*, 12 May 2000, p.22.

26.   The *Bringing Them Home* report (1997) detailed the practice of separating thousands of Aboriginal children from their families. Collectively, these children have become known as the Stolen Generations.

27.   Alan Gold, 'A sorry story: Aborigines and the Holocaust', *AJN (Melb.)*, 28 April 2000, p.13. ECAJ president Nina Bassat also attacked Heron's denial as well as a comment by Family and Community Services Minister, Senator Jocelyn Newman that comparison with the Holocaust was disgraceful; Bernard Freedman, 'Stolen generation deniers condemned', *AJN (Melb.)*, 7 April 2000, p.3.

28.   Ron Castan, 'The Great Australian Silence', *AJN (Melb.)*, 23 April 1999.

29.   Ibid.

30.   Robert Manne, quoted in Deborah Stone, 'Jogging Australia's faulty memory', *AJN (Melb.)*, 6 April 2001, p.15. Manne is prominent political writer, author of *In Denial: The Stolen Generations and the Right*, and child of pre-war Jewish refugees from Nazism. Colin Tatz, author of *Obstacle Race*, about racism in Australian sport, asserted that Australia was not worthy of hosting the Olympic Games because of the appalling conditions and treatment endured by Aborigines.

31.   Bernard Rechter, 'Howard PhD anger', Letters, *AJN (Melb.)*, 19 May 2000, p.12.

32.   ECAJ President Diane Shteinman, child of refugees from the Soviet Union, said that the Stolen Generation had been deprived of its 'precious gift of inheritance. The Inquiry started the healing process. Restitution can never compensate for the human cost of the policy, but can serve as a platform for a dignified future'; 'Government urged to back Stolen Children findings', *AJN (Syd.)*, 30 May 1997, pp.3, 12.

33.   In addition to advocacy on behalf of Australia's indigenous peoples, Jewish community organizations and individuals are beginning to provide financial support. Encouraging first steps taken include, but are not restricted to, *B'nai B'rith*'s 'Koorie Achievement Scholarships' (in conjunction with the Australia-India Society) which help Aboriginal students through their secondary schooling; *AJN (Melb.)*, 15 Jan. 1999. p.8. Individual Jews have been involved with Aboriginal communities in various ways, for example, Arnold Zable has worked with Wurundjeri elders on a number of educational projects.

34.   Involvement was not totally altruistic; there was also concern that Holocaust denier David Irving would renew his application for a visa if he perceived a new political climate in Australia; Bernard Freedman, 'Jewish leaders concerned by Howard speech', *AJN (Melb.)*, 27 Sept. 1996.

35.   Howard A. Freeman, 'Victims of history', *AJN (Melb.)*, 11 Dec., 1998, p.23. Likewise, in his keynote address at a forum on Land, Memory and Reconciliation organized by the Koori Research Centre and the Australian Centre For Jewish Civilisation at Monash University, Ron Castan realized that '[my] determination not to stand by and see the Jewish people downtrodden and persecuted was mean- ingless if I was standing by and seeing another oppressed people downtrodden and persecuted within my own country'; Ron Castan, 'The Great Australian Silence', *AJN (Melb.)*, 16 April 1999, p.15. See also Mark Lew, Letters, 'The Stolen

Generation', *AJN (Melb.)*, 19 March 1999, p.18.

36. Both Philip Mendes and Sam Lipski have identified increased Australian Jewish support for Aboriginal rights, see Philip Mendes, Letters, *AJN (Melb)*, 5 Dec. 1997, p.20; Sam Lipski, 'What Aborigines are learning from Jews, *AJN (Melb)*, 11 Aug. 2000, p.15.

37. Keshet has raised more than $250,000 over the years since 1994, much of which went to refugees, but also for various other non-Jewish social causes. In 2001 Keshet expanded the scope of its activities to include helping feed Melbourne's hungry and homeless.

38. Joshua Felman, 'Keshet raises $18,000', *AJN (Melb.)*, 6 July 2001, p.7; 'Students raise Rwanda aid', *AJN (Syd.)*, 5 Aug. 1994, p.6; Shoshana Lenthen, 'Jews respond to Rwandan crisis', *AJN (Syd.)*, 5 Aug. 1994, News/views, pp.1, 6.

39. Jackie Brygel, 'Yiddish concert to benefit refugees', *AJN (Melb.)*, 29 July 1994, p.7. Arnold Zable, *Jewels and Ashes* (Newham: Scribe, 1991).

40. Letter from a group of Moriah college students, 'Bystanders', *AJN (Syd.)*, 22 Sept. 1995, p.18.

41. Saba Feniger, 'Peace in the Balkans but refugees never forget', *AJN (Melb.)*, 18 June 1999, p.2.

42. Lila Raskin and Monique Gordon, 'Mount Scopus takes action', *AJN (Melb.)*, 4 June 1999, p.12.

43. Bernard Freedman, 'Kosovar "temporary haven" visas criticised', *AJN (Melb.)*, 7 May 1999, p.3.

44. Suzanna Rutland, 'Refugees: Let us be generous', *AJN (Melb.)*, 3 Dec. 1999, p.16. Rutland is a historian at Sydney University and daughter of pre-war refugees from Nazism.

45. Mark Briskin, 'We must not stand by', *AJN (Melb.)*, 17 Sept. 1999, p.1.

46. Angie Fox, 'Keshet appeal for starving millions', *AJN (Melb.)*, 29 Sept. 2001, p.22.

47. Victor Kleerkoper, 'Medical supplies for Timor', *AJN (Melb.)*, 25 Feb. 2000, p.19.

48. Michael Danby, 'The Indonesian Einsatz Kommandos', *AJN (Melb.)*, 24 Sept. 1999, p.16.

49. 'As teachers of the Holocaust...', *AJN (Melb.)*, 17 Oct. 1999, p.3.

50. Vic Alhadeff, 'Jews call for compassion', *AJN (Melb.)*, 7 Sept. 2001, p.1.

51. Robin Rothfield, Letters, *AJN (Melb.)*, 16 Nov. 2001, p.17. Likewise, images of shiploads of Jewish refugees attempting to flee Nazi Europe, led Rabbi Moshe Gutnick, son of Holocaust survivors, to assert that there should be no quotas for genuine refugees.

52. Sam Lipski, 'Refugees and the news we should have heard', *AJN (Melb.)*, 7 Sept. 2001, p.21.

53. Danny Gocs, 'Arts concert for refugees', *AJN (Melb.)*, 12 Oct. 2001, p.18.

54. Mark Baker, 'Rocking the boat: why I protested against the PM', *AJN (Melb.)*, 14 Sept. 2001, p.17.

55. John Rosenberg, 'Ashamed Australian', Letters, *AJN (Melb.)*, 26 Oct. 2001, p.14.

56. Danya Levy, 'Plea for asylum-seekers', *AJN (Melb.)*, 8 Feb. 2002, p.9; Marcus Einfeld, 'Restoring dignity to the world', *AJN (Melb.)*, 5 April 2002, p.18; Bernard Freedman, 'Rethink Woomera, urges community', *AJN (Melb.)*, 1 Feb. 2002, p.1.

57. Freedman, 'Rethink Woomera, urges community'.

58. Alana Rosenbaum, 'Beyond the barbed wire', *AJN (Melb.)*, 8 Feb. 2002, p.15.

59. Arnold Zable, 'The horror of detention', *AJN (Melb.)*, 1 Feb. 2002, p.19.

60. Ibid; 'Child survivors fight for detained children', *AJN (Melb.)*, 18 May 2001, p.4; Alana Rosenbaum, 'Caring for the stranger', *AJN (Melb.)*, 23 Nov. 2001, p.4. Robert Richter QC, a civil liberties lawyer, likewise tied his involvement in refugee issues to his parents' refugee legacy.

61. Paul Valent, quoted in 'Child survivors fight for detained children', *AJN (Melb.)*,

18 May 2001, p.4; Alana Rosenbaum, 'Through the eyes of a refugee', *AJN (Melb.)*, 19 April 2002, p.10. Valent is also President of the Australasian Society for Traumatic Stress Studies and member of the Independent Detention Advisory Committee that monitored conditions in the detention centres.

62.   Holocaust survivor Rabbi Chaim Gutnick issued a statement of support: 'We who have felt what it means to be strangers, homeless, and refugees for so many years must be in the forefront to sympathise and support those refugees who are in a similar position today'; Alana Rosenbaum, 'Orthodox, Progressives rally for refugees', *AJN (Melb.)*, 5 April 2002, p.35.

63.   Jewish Youth for Refugees is a non-political, humanitarian-focused coalition organised by Skif youth group; Monique Hain, 'Once were strangers', Letters, *AJN (Melb.)*, 29 March 2002, p.16; Alana Rosenbaum, 'Pesach rally for asylum-seekers', *AJN (Melb.)*, 8 March 2002, p.3; Rosenbaum, 'Orthodox, Progressives rally for refugees'.

64.   Alana Rosenbaum, 'Uniting in the fight for refugees', *AJN (Melb.)*, 12 April 2002, p.26; Alana Rosenbaum, 'Jews, Muslims in succah refuge at Maribyrnong', *AJN (Melb.)*, 4 Oct. 2002, p.6.

65.   Alana Rosenbaum, 'Jews, Muslims in succah refuge at Maribyrnong', *AJN (Melb.)*, 4 Oct. 2002, p.6. This chapter aims to provide a sample of individuals and organizations involved in supporting refugees rights in Australia. Other activists include, but are not limited to, members of NSW Jewish Board of Deputies Social Justice Committee, Jewish Care, Temple Emanuel's Social Justice Committee and JET (Jews for Ethnic Tolerance).

66.   George Greenberg, 'Safe haven', Letters, *AJN (Melb.)*, 8 March 2002, p.16.

67.   For example see, Paul Winter, 'I dislike it', Letters, *AJN (Melb.)*, 15 Feb. 2002, p.16.

68.   Erwin Lamm quoted in Alana Rosenbaum, 'Jews for Refugees gathers coalition for Maribyrnong rally', *AJN (Melb.)*, 22 March 2002, p.4. See also Sam Blumenstein, 'Pertinent questions', Letters, *AJN (Melb.)*, 5 April 2002, p.29.

69.   For example, see Blumenstein, 'Pertinent questions'.

70.   Bill Rubinstein, 'Unemployable refugees', Letters, *AJN (Melb.)*, 22 March 2002, p.16; Alana Rosenbaum, 'Historian slams stance on asylum-seekers', *AJN (Melb.)*, 1 March 2002, p.6.

71.   Michael Burd, 'Stop the ME refugees', Letters, *AJN (Melb.)*, 22 Feb. 2002, p.16

72   Dan Same, 'Peace-loving Muslims', *AJN (Melb.)*, 15 Feb. 2002, p.16. See also, 'Refugees are humans', *AJN (Melb.)*, 12 April 2002, p.16; Editorial, *AJN (Melb.)*, 21 Sept. 2001, p.14.

73.   David Zyngier, quoted in Alana Rosenbaum, 'Refugees and Israel: conflict of interest?', *AJN (Melb.)*, 19 April 2002, p.6. See also Peter Kohn, Letters, *AJN (Melb.)*, 12 April 2001, p.16.

74.   The question of whether Jewish universalism and Jewish survival can coexist remains at the forefront of contemporary Jewish debates, but beyond the confines of this chapter.

75.   Grahame Leonard, quoted in Alana Rosenbaum, 'Refugees and Israel: conflict of interest?' *AJN (Melb.)*, 19 April 2002, p.6.

76.   Vic Alhadeff and Alana Rosenbaum, 'Leaders stay away from asylum protests', *AJN (Melb.)*, 29 March 2002, p.7. This is not the first time that Jews have avoided participation in progressive causes due to the anti-Zionism of the extreme left. An additional reason for non-attendance was that the rally took place during Pesach.

77.   It should be pointed out that this more universalist orientation of Australian Jewry is limited; absent from Jewish community's main areas of involvement in Australian society are such central social issues, as poverty, drugs and welfare reform, gay rights and gender issues. I thank Philip Mendes for pointing out some of these absences.

78.   Chantal Abitbol, 'Anne Frank Trust seeks Aussie ties', *AJN (Melb.)*, 25 Jan. 2002, p.10.

CHAPTER 7

1.   W. D. Rubinstein, *A History of the Jews in the English-Speaking World: Great Britain* (London: Macmillan, 1996), pp.6–7.
2.   Kitia Altman, 'Commemoration of *Yom HaShoah*', *Centre News*, 7, 3 (Sept. 1990), p.4.
3.   Judith Hassan, personal communication, 4 July 2003; Ruth Goodman, personal communication, 29 June 2003.

Index

Gathering of Jewish Holocaust Survivors (Washington) (1983), 16, 23; American Jewish leadership, 15; Holocaust Memorial Museum, 2, 16, 31, 34; Jewish community in, 3; National Days of Remembrance, 2; 9/11 terrorist attacks, 100–1

United Synagogue (Britain), 12, 13, 67

universality of Holocaust, 9, 35, 36, 42, 48, 52, 106

Ur, Doron, 23

usable pasts, concept of, 10

Valenci, Lucette, 70

Valent, Paul, 102

Valley of Bones, 63

Valley of the Lost communities project, 27

Vatican, 38

Verrall, Richard, 27–8

'Victims' Day', 79

Victorian Award for Excellence in Multicultural Affairs (2002), 49

Victorian Jewish Board of Deputies, Jewish Heritage Committee, 75

Wachtell, H., 73

Wagerman, Jo, 80

Waldheim affair, 16

Walnes, Gillian, 105

War Memorial Museum (Auckland), 19, 50

Warsaw Ghetto Uprising, 11–12, 41; Commemorations, 18, 44, 74, 75, 81; exhibition on, 13; heroes, 58; heroism, 36–7; and

martyrdom, 67; Memorial organizing committee, 82, 83

Wasserman, Alec, 40

Weinberger, Alex, 84

Weiner Library, 29

Wellington Jewish Community Centre, 17, 51

Wertheim, Peter, 14–15

West Bank, Israeli Defence Force, 61; war on terror, 61

Wiener, Bono, 21, 25

Wiesel, Elie, 24

Wilkomirski scandal, 31

Wolski, Sam, 42–3

Woomera Detention Centre for illegal immigrants to Australia, 59–60

World Jewish Congress, 71

Wright, Susanne, 49

Wyman, David, 4

Yad Vashem, 21, 27; Holocaust Martyrs' and Heroes Memorial Authority, 68

Yad Vashem Committee UK (YVCUK), 27, 28, 29, 75

Yahrzeit candles, 71

Yehoshua, A. B., 90

Yerushalmi, Yosef Hayim, 71

Yom ha'Atzmaut (Israeli Independence Day), 84, 87

Yom haShoah (Holocaust Day) commemorations, 1, 2, 9, 36, 38, 56, 72–6; Australia, 13, 23, 39, 40, 41, 42, 46, 62, 73; Britain, 38, 44, 73, 75; definitions, 12; Jewish tradition, derived from, 70, 71; *Kadish* recited at, 74; as 'Martyrs Memorial Day', 68; Minutes/Annual Reports, 8;